INSIGHTS

Phonics in Context

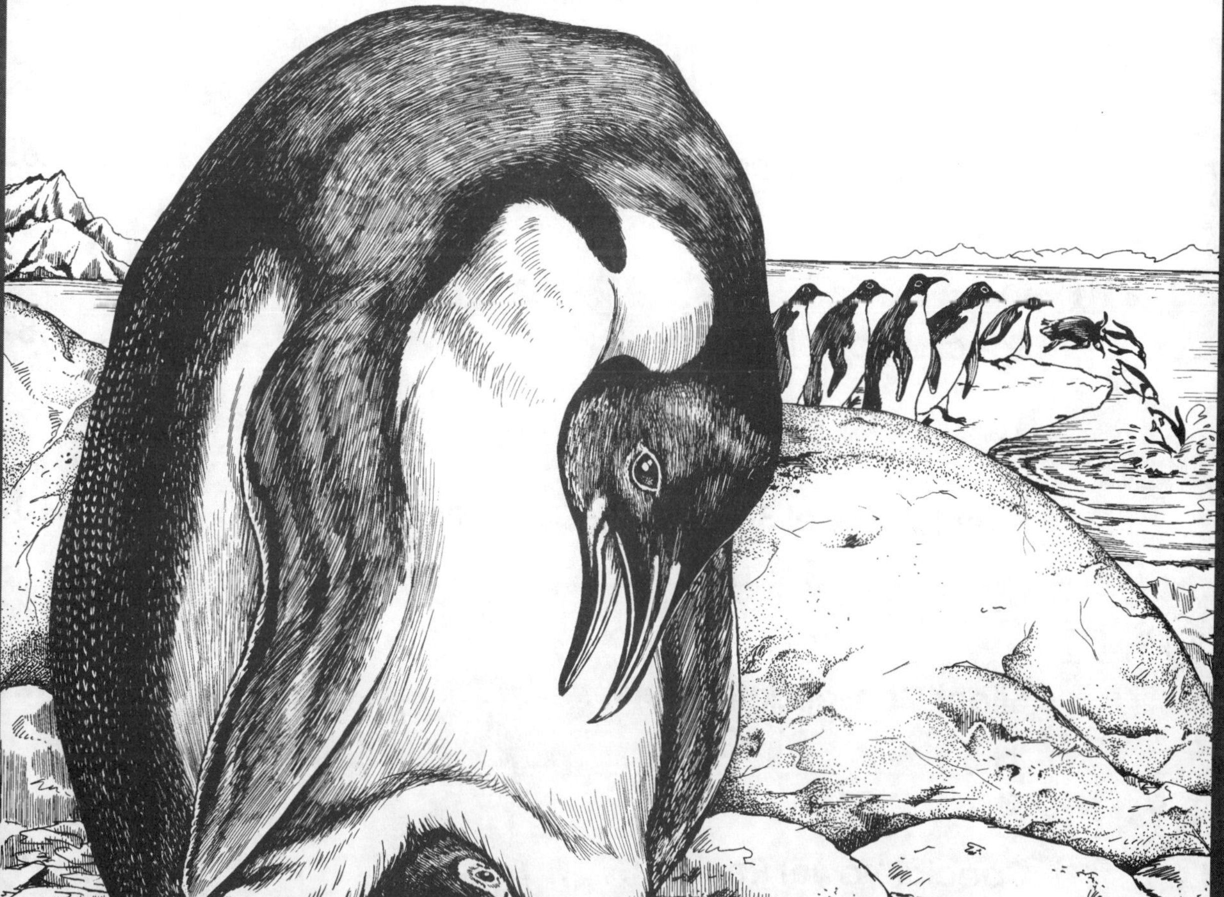

READING AS THINKING

CONTENTS

Send permission requests to: Charlesbridge Publishing, 85 Main Street, Watertown, Massachusetts 02472.
www.charlesbridge.com

Printed in the United States of America.

ISBN: 1-57091-072-3

10 9

My name is ______________________________.

Circle the vowel sound you hear.

a e i o u

1.	a	e	i	o	u
2.	a	e	i	o	u
3.	a	e	i	o	u
4.	a	e	i	o	u
5.	a	e	i	o	u
6.	a	e	i	o	u
7.	a	e	i	o	u
8.	a	e	i	o	u
9.	a	e	i	o	u
10.	a	e	i	o	u

My name is ____.

Complete each word by adding a vowel to make the picture name.

My name is ______________________________.

Complete each word by adding a vowel to make the picture name.

My name is ________________.

Circle the picture named by the word.

a e i o u

1. bag	2. net	3. hit
4. map	5. cup	6. cat
7. bell	8. chick	9. cab

My name is ______________________.

Circle the picture named by the word.

My name is ______________________________.

Complete each sentence with the best word.

1. On the road Jack __________ three trolls.
met mat

2. Little Tina could not sit in the __________ chair.
big bug

3. The shiny star was __________ from gold paper.
cot cut

4. Will you __________ the stamp for the letter?
lick lock

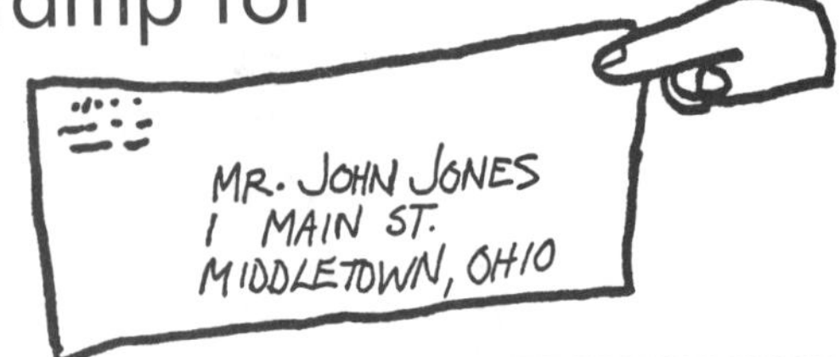

5. Fred put the apples in a __________ .
sick sack

My name is ______________________________.

Complete each sentence with the best word.

1. Our puppy __________ a hole in my shoe.

bit bat

2. My mom has a blue ink __________.

pen pan

3. The cat took a nap on the __________.

rag rug

4. This plant needs a new __________.

pot pit

5. The train is going down the __________.

trick track

My name is ________________________________.

Circle the word that completes each sentence.
Write the word on the line.

a e i o u

1. I like to use a __________ when it is hot.
fan fun

2. Please __________ me play with that toy.
let lot

3. It is __________ when the sun comes out.
hat hot

4. Sue was __________ when she lost the game.
sad sod

5. Did you dig a __________ in the mud?
pit pet

6. What did you __________ at the store?
get got

My name is ______________________________.

Circle the word that completes each sentence.
Write the word on the line.

1. He ran so ____________ he won the race.

   fast fist

2. I like the water in my ____________ nice and hot.

   tub tab

3. There is a hole in my ____________.

   sick sock

4. I want to ____________ in my warm bed.

   rust rest

5. I like the music the ____________ plays.

   band bend

My name is ______________________________________.

Circle the word that completes each sentence.
Write the word on the line.

1. Sheila played in the _______________ at the beach.
send sand

2. Wow! We sure got _______________ in the rain.
wit wet

3. Use the _______________ to clean up the spill.
mop map

4. Jim and I like to catch _______________ .
bags bugs

5. I love to _______________ my new puppy.
pat pot

Cut out this wheel.
Put it inside the big wheel.

My name is ____.

Turn the small wheel and match the short vowel sounds you hear. Write the words on the lines at the bottom.

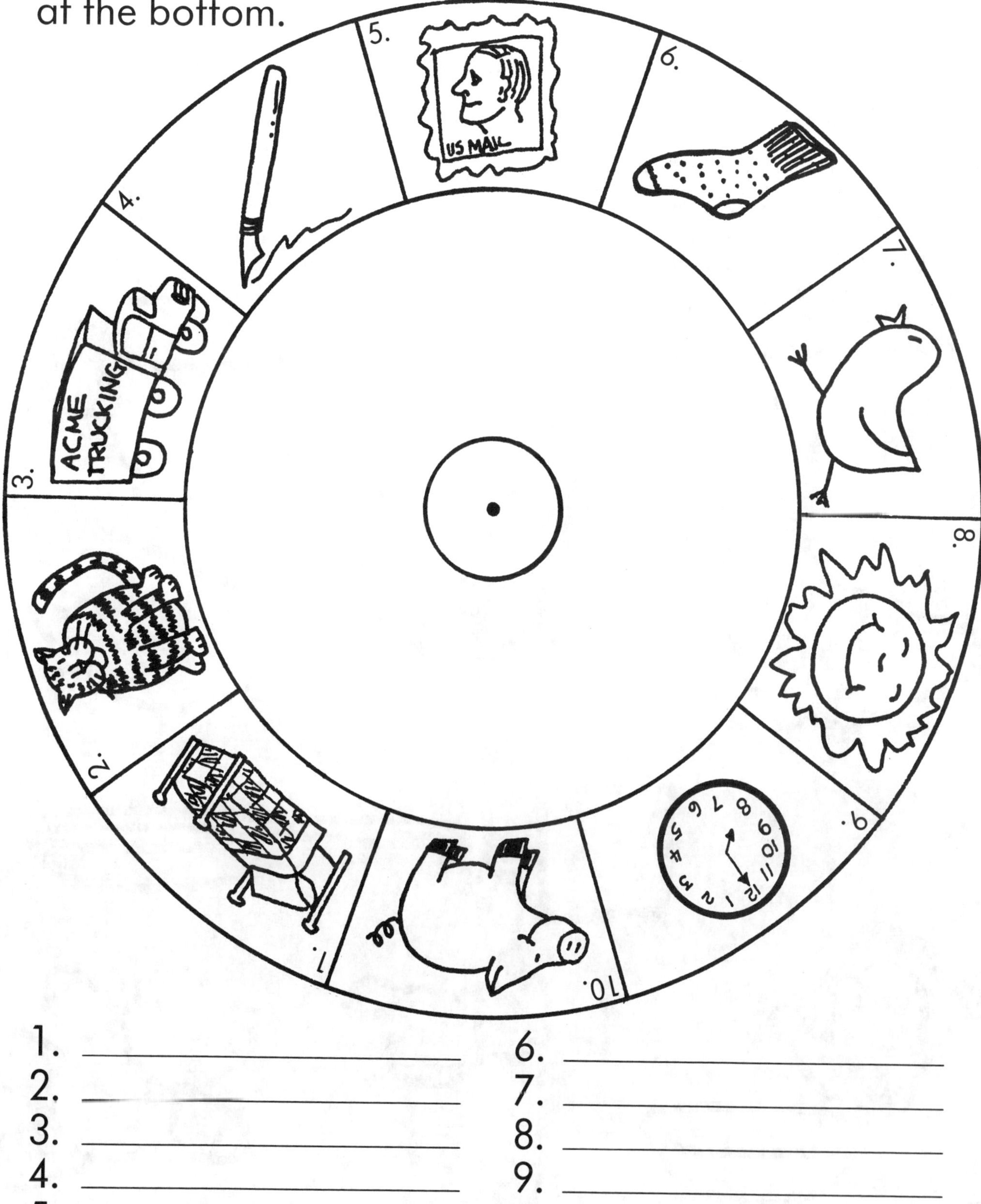

1. ______________________ 6. ______________________
2. ______________________ 7. ______________________
3. ______________________ 8. ______________________
4. ______________________ 9. ______________________
5. ______________________ 10. ______________________

My name is ______________________________.

Read the directions. Add to each picture.

Put some socks on the fox.
Make some lips on the fish.
Make a duck swim in the cup.
Give the hen, chickens ten.
Put some chips in the dish.
Draw a mask for the cat.
Put a lock on the box.
Cook some ham in the pan.
Make the puppy look funny.
Put little Teddy in a bed.

Dear Parent or Guardian:

This year we are using the *Phonics in Context* book of *INSIGHTS: Reading as Thinking* to review letter shapes and sounds. We have just completed the first unit which is a review of five vowel sounds: **a** as in **apple**, **e** as in **egg**, **i** as in **insect**, **o** as in **octopus**, and **u** as in **umbrella**. The purpose of phonic strategies is to help students sound out words so that they can figure out the meaning.

As parents and teachers of young children, we share a common goal: to help children become successful readers. In order to achieve this goal, we teach them phonic and comprehension strategies and help them develop their interest in reading. During this school year, I will be sending home with your child a series of letters and reading lists that I hope you will find interesting and useful. Some letters suggest activities that you and your child might enjoy together. Some of these activities are linked directly to our classroom, others focus on broader applications of beginning reading.

The book list on the back of each letter includes just a few of the many wonderful children's books in your local library for you and your child to share. Reading at home is a wonderful gift you can give your child. I look forward to meeting with you this year to discuss your child's progress.

Sincerely,

Your Child's Teacher

Literature List

Barrett, Joyce Durham. *Willie's Not the Hugging Kind.* HarperCollins, 1989. When Willie's friends decide that hugging is silly, he decides to stop hugging everybody, too.

Browne, Anthony. *Gorilla.* Knopf, 1983. A girl who loves gorillas receives a birthday present that is better than she expected.

Greenfield, Eloise. *Nathaniel Talking.* Black Butterfly, 1989. Nine-year-old Nathaniel talks about his life, his family, and his thoughts in 18 rhythmic poems.

Horenstein, Henry. *Sam Goes Trucking.* Houghton Mifflin, 1989. Sam learns exactly what a sixteen-wheeler can do when he spends a day with his father who is a trucker.

Jonas, Ann. *Aardvarks, Disembark.* Greenwillow, 1990. After the zebras get off Noah's ark, dozens of strange creatures from addaxes to zorils follow them down Mt. Ararat.

Kellogg, Steven. *Ralph's Secret Weapon.* Dial Press, 1983. Ralph's eccentric aunt decides that his bassoon lessons make him the right person to help stop a giant sea serpent from terrorizing the United States.

Kroll, Steven. *Big Jeremy.* Holiday, 1989. Jeremy only wants to help his friendly neighbors, but being a giant makes that difficult for him.

Ormerod, Jan. *The Story of Chicken Licken.* Lothrop, 1986. This retelling of the chicken little story is presented as a play with costumed actors and audience in the background.

My name is ________________________________.

Circle the letters that complete the words.
Write the letters on the lines.

My name is ____________________________________.

Circle the letters that complete the words.
Write the letters on the lines.

My name is ______________________________________.

Say the sound you hear at the beginning of each word.
Write the sound on the lines below the picture.

sp	sc	sn	sm	sk	sw

My name is ______________________________.

Circle the letters that complete each word.
Write the letters on the lines.

My name is ______________________________.

Circle the letters that complete each word.
Write the letters on the lines.

My name is ______________________________________.

Say the ending sound of each word.
Write the ending sound you hear on the lines below the pictures.

ld	pt	lt	mp	nd

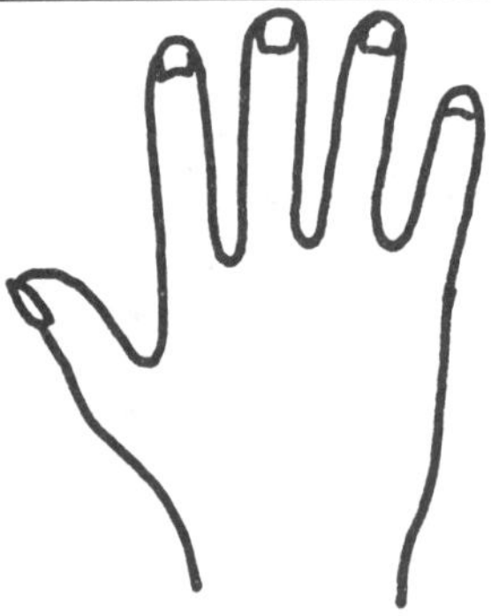

My name is ______________________________.

Write the consonant blend in the spaces to complete each word.

1. The ___y is very blue today.

2. Amy did not want to be ___all. She wanted to be very tall.

3. There is no ice. We cannot ice ___ate today.

4. I like to ___im under the water.

5. A ___amp is a wet and muddy place.

6. I like to run, hop, and ___ip.

7. I like to ___ile at funny things.

8. "Put on your blue ___eater. It's cold," Mom said.

9. We could see the ___oke from the fire.

My name is ______________________________.

Write the consonant blend in the spaces to complete each word.

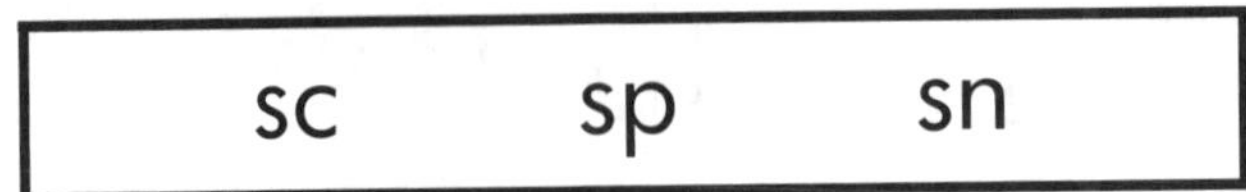

sc sp sn

1. A ___arf is a good thing to put on in the winter.

2. Some people are afraid of ___akes. I am not.

3. Robin wants to go to the moon. She wants to go to outer ___ace.

4. He started to ___ore as soon as he fell asleep.

5. I am a monster. I can ___are you!

6. I will ___end my money on a new book.

7. It was cold and the sky was gray. It started to ___ow.

8. The ___ore was 4 to 0. Our team was winning!

9. I think that ___aghetti is the best food in the world.

My name is ____.

Write the blend to complete each word.

ld	pt	lt	mp	nd

1. It was snowing and the wind was blowing hard. I was co___.

2. This sta___ was on a letter from my grandmother.

3. Jim sle___ on the grass when we went camping.

4. It was ki___ of Linda to take care of the puppy.

5. The ring was go___ and had a blue stone in it.

6. It was not my fau___ that we could not go.

7. We could ju___ very far if we were on the moon.

8. Dad swe___ the floor of the cabin with a broom.

9. The sou___ of the wind made us want to go inside.

10. The snow on the mountain started to me___ in the spring.

My name is ______________________________.

Circle the letters that complete each word.
Write the letters on the lines.

My name is ______________________________.

Write the letters to complete each word.

wr	kn	ph	gh

1. ___ite your name on the back of your picture.
2. When the tele___one rings, my brother always answers it.
3. Sally heard a ___ock on the door. "Come in," she said.
4. Two plus two equals five gives the ___ong answer.
5. Do not give me any more. I have enou___.
6. The blanket is very soft and smooth. It is not rou___ .
7. We started to lau___ at the funny story.
8. Dad does not ___ow the answer.
9. Use your ___ife to cut the rope.
10. ___ilip is a boy's name.

write	Philip	enough	wrong
telephone	knock	knife	rough
know			laugh

My name is ________________________________.

Your teacher will read the picture names. Circle the sound you hear in two of the words in each picture box.

My name is ____________________________________.

Your teacher will read the picture names. Circle the sound you hear in two of the words in each picture box.

My name is ____.

9.
lt ld nd
10.
mp pt ph
11.
USA
75¢
nd lt mp
12.
HA HA
mp wr gh
13.
nd mp ld
14.
ld lt ph
15.
ld pt ph

My name is ____________________________________.

Circle the word with the same blend as the first word.

spot	stop	spoke	snake
smell	snap	scare	smoke
swan	swim	smile	snip
snake	small	snail	spill
scare	snug	score	smack
wrong	wing	wrinkle	wink
knee	knife	kick	kite
salt	black	built	nail
cold	last	clear	told
wept	water	dry	swept
camp	snap	lamp	score
sand	small	knife	find

My name is ______________________.

Color each bubble with a pair of blends or digraphs.

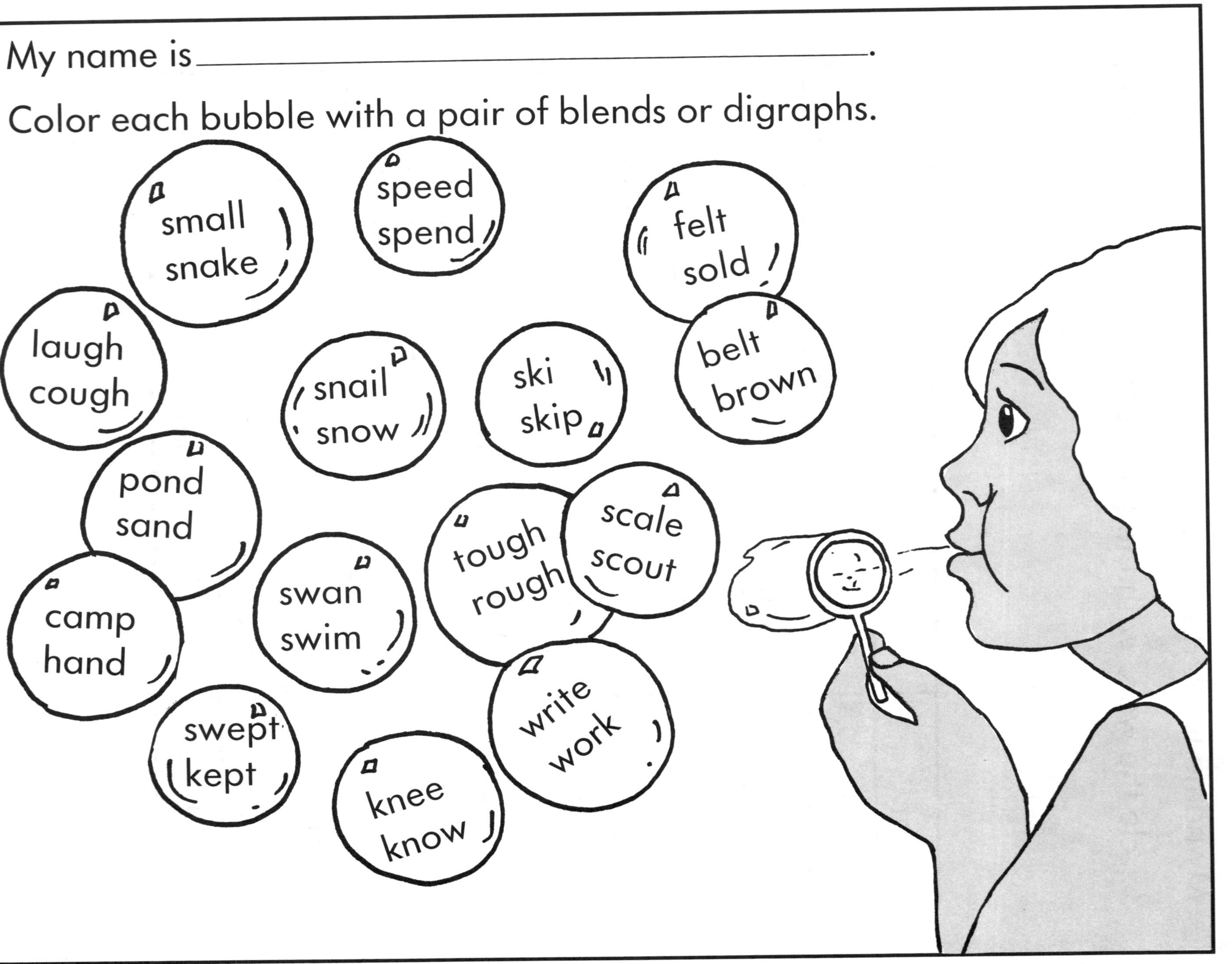

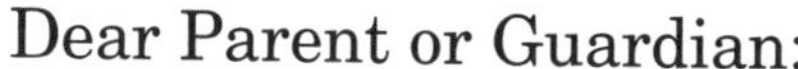

Dear Parent or Guardian:

We have just completed the second unit of *Phonics in Context* which is part of the program *INSIGHTS: Reading as Thinking*. In this unit we studied consonant blends and digraphs.

sp as in **spot**	**sw** as in **swim**	**ld** as in **gold**
sk as in **skip**	**sn** as in **sneeze**	**lt** as in **melt**
sc as in **scoop**	**sm** as in **smile**	**pt** as in **kept**
wr as in **wrist**	**ph** as in **phone** or **graph**	**mp** as in **camp**
kn as in **knee**	**gh** as in **ghost** or **laugh**	**nd** as in **sand**

There are many ways you can help your child develop an interest in and a love of reading. Children who have their own books often enjoy reading them over and over again. Let friends and relatives know that books are an appropriate gift. When a new book arrives, look at it together to develop an idea of the treat to come when you sit down together to read it.

The local library is also a source of books on every subject in which your child might be interested. It's a good idea to set aside a regular time each day for reading. Several research studies show that just reading your child a bedtime story each night can significantly improve his or her reading. Best of all, reading together can be a special, rewarding time for both parents and children.

While you are reading a bedtime story, stop at each word with a consonant blend or digraph and ask your child to read it. The books listed on the back of this letter include blends and digraphs and are also great fun to read.

Sincerely,

Your Child's Teacher

Literature List

Allard, Harry. *Miss Nelson Has a Field Day* and *Miss Nelson is Missing*. Houghton Mifflin, 1985. Class 207 doesn't appreciate Miss Nelson until a vile substitute teacher shows up.

Bang, Molly. *The Paper Crane*. Greenwillow, 1985. A paper crane comes to life and brings prosperity in this modern retelling of an old story.

Enderle, Judith Ross and Stephanie Gordon. *Six Snowy Sheep*. Boyds Mill, 1994. In earlier books, the sheep were sleepy and creepy. In this one, they have a Christmas adventure.

Fox, Mem. *Sophie*. Harcourt, 1994. An African-American family story of three generations told with gentle warmth.

Livingston, Myra Cohn. *Space Songs*. Holiday House, 1988. Outer space is brought much closer through this collection of poems.

MacLachlan, Patricia. *The Sick Day*. Pantheon 1979. Emily's father takes care of everything the day she gets a "stomach ache in her head."

McPhail, David. *Moony B. Finch, the Fastest Draw in the West*. Artists, 1994. A humorous story of a boy who saves the day with his artwork and fast thinking.

Ryan, Pam Muñoz. *The Flag We Love*. Charlesbridge, 1995. The story of our flag, what it represents, and how to show respect for it.

Steig, William. *Roland, the Minstrel Pig*. Windmill Books, 1968. Sebastian is a scheming fox who finds Roland and his singing voice sweet enough to eat.

Turkle, Brinton. *Do Not Open*. Dutton, 1981. Treasure hunting with her cat on the beach after a big storm, Miss Moody finds a mysterious bottle and listens to the voice within that pleads with her to pull the stopper.

My name is ______________________________.

Write the missing vowel letter for each picture.

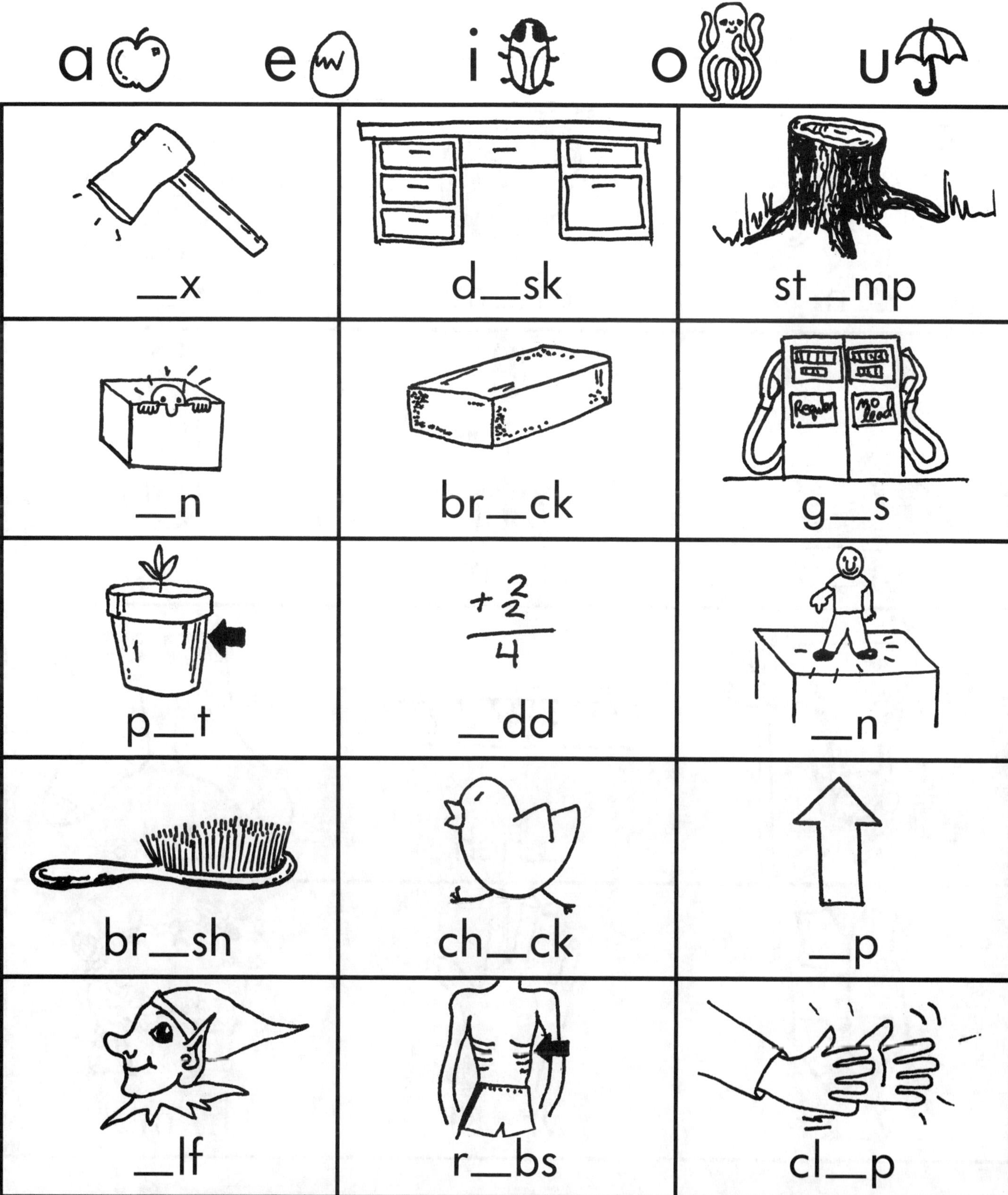

My name is ______________________________.

Write the missing vowel letter for each picture.

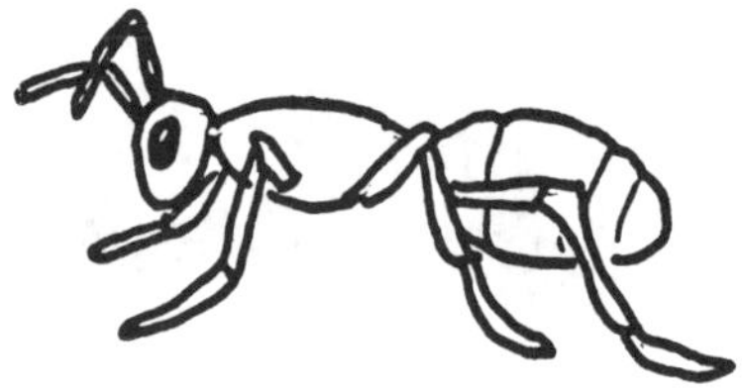 __nt	 pl__m	 cr__b
 m__p	 st__m	 cl__p
 __x	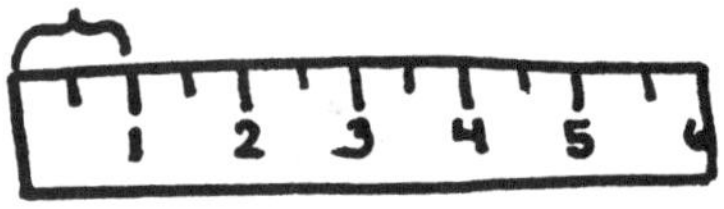 __nch	 s__cks
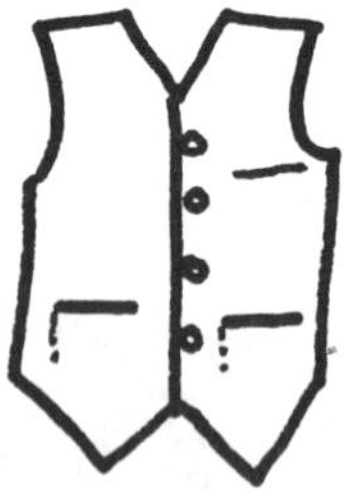 v__st	 wr__st	 l__mb

My name is ______________________________________.

Write the short vowel word on the line to complete each sentence. Find two more words in each sentence with short vowel sounds. Write the words on the lines under the sentence.

1. Mother will ____________ up the rolls and cake.

mix make ________ ________

2. Last Friday we had a ______________ in school.

play test ________ ________

3. That ___________ looks like a big bird in the sky.

jet kite ________ ________

4. The man hit the tree with a big ______________ .

iron ax ________ ________

5. Please stay ______________ the bus until it stops.

on by ________ ________

6. We like to ________________ apples in the fall.

pick eat ________ ________

7. Dad sat the baby on his ____________________.

chair lap ________ ________

8. Pam always ______________ her doll before she goes to bed.

hugs needs ________ ________

9. Do you know how long an ________________ is?

inch mile ________ ________

10. Bill got a ____________ on his head when he fell down on the playground.

leaf lump ________ ________

My name is ______________________________.

Draw a line through the pictures that have a long vowel sound.

a as in ape **e** as in easy **i** as in ice
o as in ocean **u** as in use

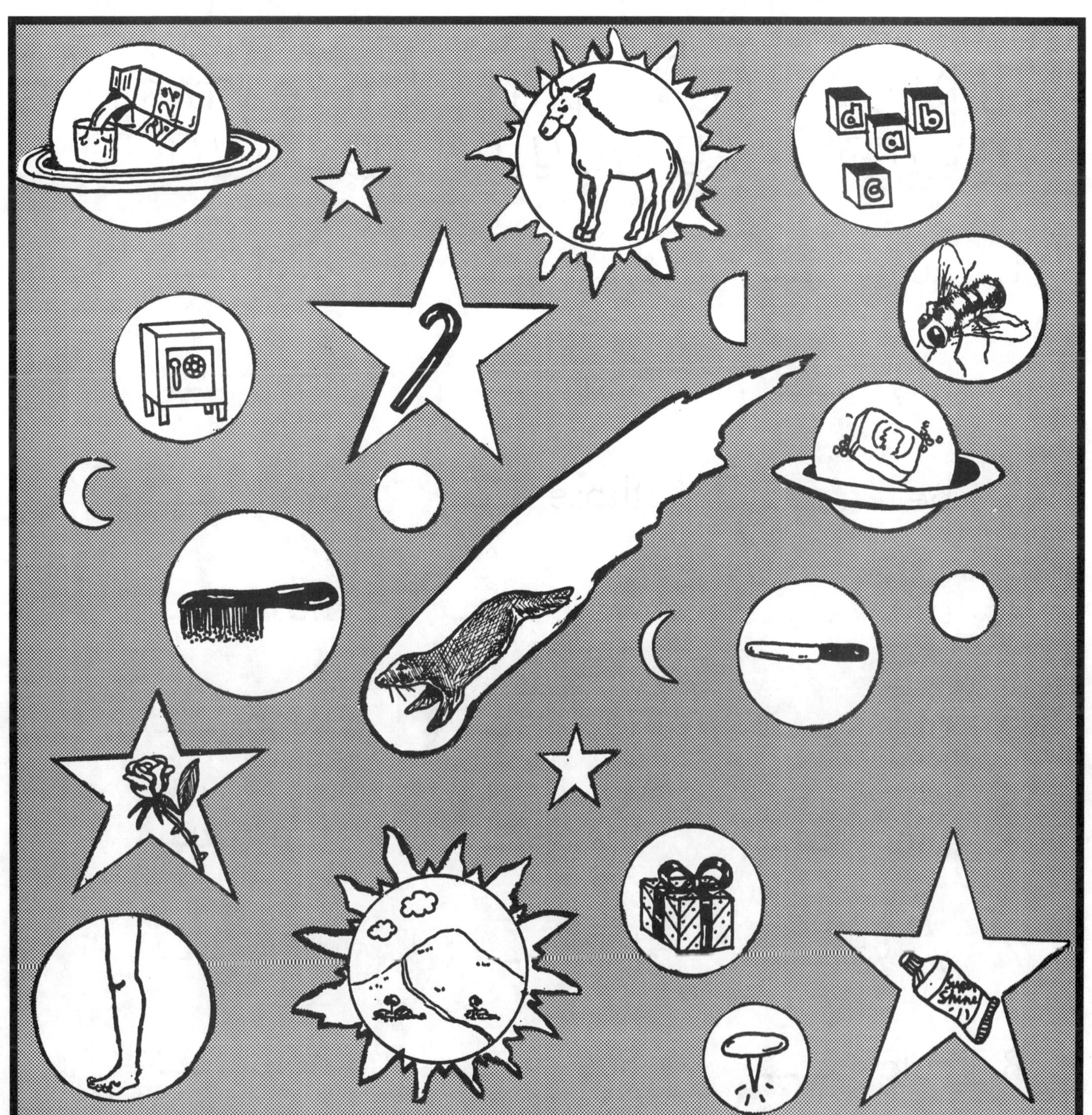

My name is ______________________________.

Write **1, 2,** or **3** on the line to show the long vowel rule you would use to read the word.

1. need ___	bite ___	coal ___
2. hay ___	sea ___	use ___
3. be ___	those ___	wait ___
4. suit ___	write ___	no ___
5. ate ___	so ___	keep ___
6. pie ___	toe ___	fire ___
7. yo-yo ___	heat ___	road ___
8. rule ___	Sue ___	hole ___

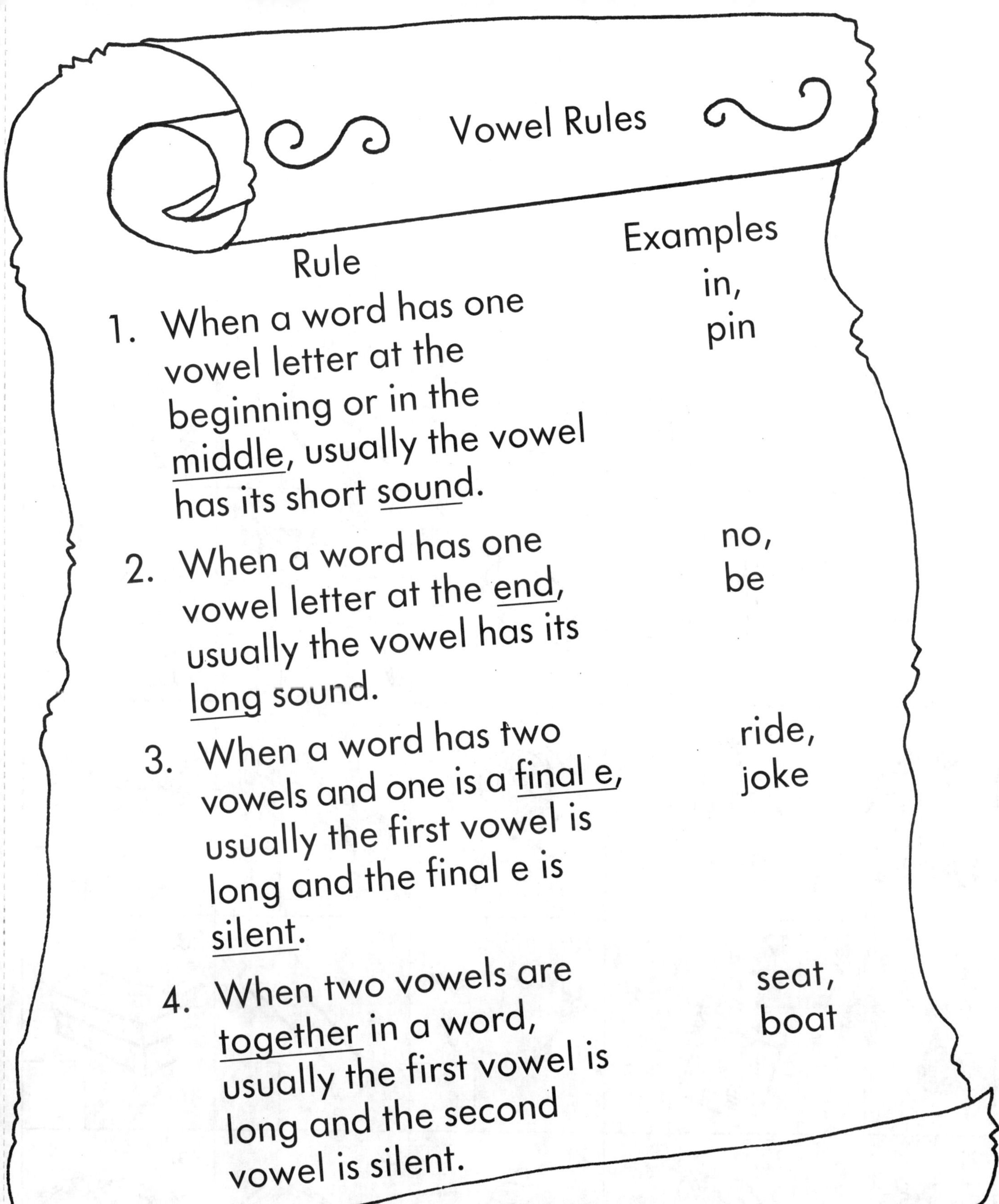

Vowel Rules

Rule	Examples
1. When a word has one vowel letter at the beginning or in the middle, usually the vowel has its short sound.	in, pin
2. When a word has one vowel letter at the end, usually the vowel has its long sound.	no, be
3. When a word has two vowels and one is a final e, usually the first vowel is long and the final e is silent.	ride, joke
4. When two vowels are together in a word, usually the first vowel is long and the second vowel is silent.	seat, boat

My name is ______________________________.

Write the letter **S** for the short vowel sound.
Write the letter **L** for the long vowel sound.

My name is ______________________________.

Read the story. Complete the chart.

Trouble for Joe

Joe did not rush home from school this day. He was sure his parents were going to be upset with him. He had a note from his teacher. The note was about singing. Joe had not done any singing during music class for the last three weeks. He did not know why. He just did not want to! He had to take the note home. Mom had to put her name on it. Joe felt sad. Then, he thought, "I am going to turn over a new leaf."

Word	Vowel Sound	Rule
Joe	long o	4
home		
this		
be		
with		
note		
three		
He		
name		
sad		
leaf		

My name is ______________________________.

Read the sentences. Underline the words in which **y** has a long **e** sound.
Circle the words in which **y** has a long **i** sound.

1. There are many cars on a city street.

2. Why did you cry when you won the pony?

3. Please try to carry the bags.

4. At eight o'clock the library was empty.

5. Every evening we sit by the window.

6. The rabbit jumped quickly over the dry leaves.

7. The smoke from the chimney curled up into the sky.

8. Are you ready to hear a funny story?

9. He is grateful for anyone who will try to help him.

10. The tiny baby was very sleepy.

My name is ______________________________.

Color the section red if the **y** in the word has a long **e** sound. Color the section yellow if the **y** in the word has a long **i** vowel sound.

cherr**y** red

sk**y** yellow

My name is ______________________________.

Write the missing vowel letter.
Put an X on the number of the vowel rule.

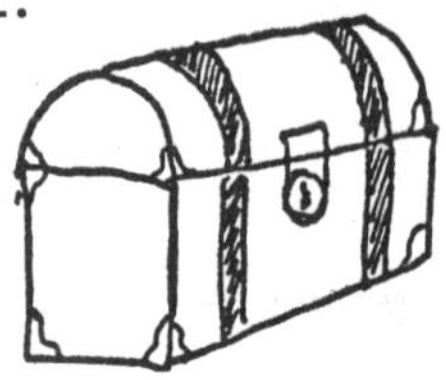

1. f_ce	2. tr_nk	3. c_at	4. b_nk
1 2 3 4	1 2 3 4	1 2 3 4	1 2 3 4
5. b_nch	6. _nt	7. _ce	8. f_et
1 2 3 4	1 2 3 4	1 2 3 4	1 2 3 4
9. n_	10. n_ts	11. wh_at	12. g_
1 2 3 4	1 2 3 4	1 2 3 4	1 2 3 4
13. s_ap	14. c_t	15. s_it	16. r_ng
1 2 3 4	1 2 3 4	1 2 3 4	1 2 3 4

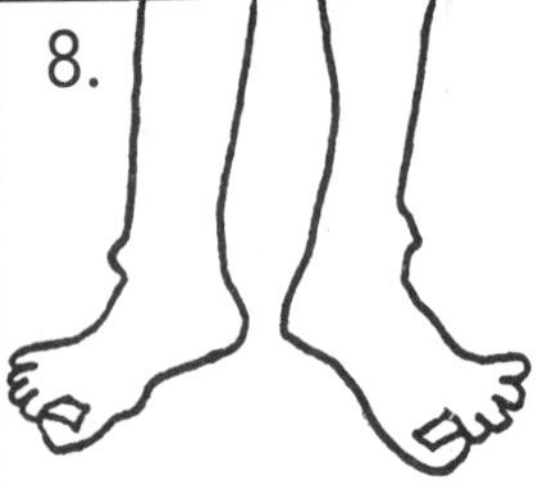

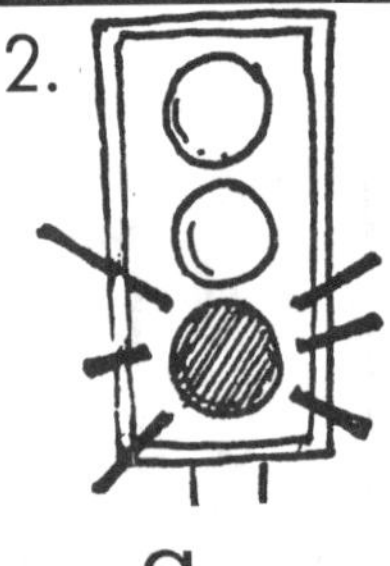

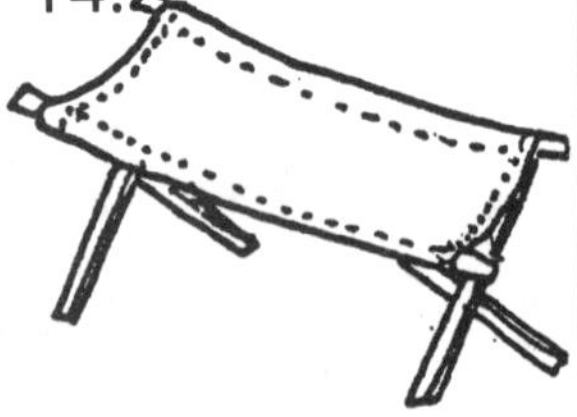

My name is ______________________________________.

Read the words in each box. Write the word that will complete each sentence.

job jab	1. My dad has a new ______________ . Do not poke and ______________ at your spinach.
fin fine	2. This is a ______________ day to go for a walk in the park. A ______________ helps a fish to swim.
add odd	3. That hat looks __________ on your head. Babies do not know how to __________ .
hi ho	4. I always say ______________ to my friends. " ______________ , ho!" said the clown.
jelly jolly	5. It's fun to be with someone __________ . Would you like apple ______________ on your bread?
best beast	6. May had on her ______________ dress at the party. An animal is called a ______________ .
cut cute	7. Puppies are so ______________ ! Ted can't ______________ on the line.

My name is ______________________________________.

Circle the word in each row that has the same vowel sound as the first word.

1. streets	jet	these	straight
2. slip	pine	lie	inch
3. nice	lie	list	nail
4. paint	ant	cave	fan
5. less	egg	heel	leaf
6. shy	ready	satisfy	study
7. ill	ripe	I	tip
8. nod	clock	oak	note
9. drove	drop	fox	oats
10. city	happy	by	yes

My name is ______________________________.

Darken the circle in front of the word that has the same vowel sound as the underlined vowel.

1. dry
   - ○ cherry
   - ○ dime
   - ○ friend

2. paint
   - ○ safe
   - ○ ask
   - ○ can

3. city
   - ○ egg
   - ○ vest
   - ○ really

4. five
   - ○ quick
   - ○ in
   - ○ by

5. rag
   - ○ late
   - ○ act
   - ○ fed

6. sleep
   - ○ bean
   - ○ tent
   - ○ herd

7. oak
   - ○ tooth
   - ○ clock
   - ○ bone

8. brush
   - ○ use
   - ○ up
   - ○ fur

9. neck
   - ○ each
   - ○ pear
   - ○ desk

10. ax
    - ○ boat
    - ○ whale
    - ○ ant

11. so
    - ○ rode
    - ○ clock
    - ○ soft

12. rule
    - ○ cup
    - ○ July
    - ○ quiet

13. its
    - ○ dive
    - ○ I'm
    - ○ drip

14. say
    - ○ pat
    - ○ wait
    - ○ army

15. dumb
    - ○ four
    - ○ rule
    - ○ must

16. candy
    - ○ hungry
    - ○ why
    - ○ your

ape
apple
easy
1
+1
2
egg
ice
insect
ocean
octopus
unicorn
umbrella

My name is ______________________________.

Circle the word that completes each sentence.

1. Mother knows a lot / lit about cars.

2. Bob gets a new ball and bet / bat every spring.

3. Dad had a mop / map in his coat pocket.

4. My dog wants me to put / pat him on the head.

5. Are you going to stop / step this playing around?

6. At / It ten o'clock I will knock on your door.

7. The frog sat on a bumpy leg / log in the pond.

8. My new coat is ten / tan.

My name is ______________________________.

Read each sentence and the words at the bottom of the page. Write the word on the line that completes each sentence.

1. When will you ______________ home for dinner?

2. ________ put on her new blue jeans this morning.

3. Curly, my dog, was ____________ glad to see me.

4. _________ has that radio with him all of the time.

5. I say hello, not __________ , to my grandparents.

6. ________________ all shouted the cheer together.

7. Give ______________________ change for the bus.

go	be	hi	so	no	he	she	me	we

My name is ____.

Write in the missing vowel letters.

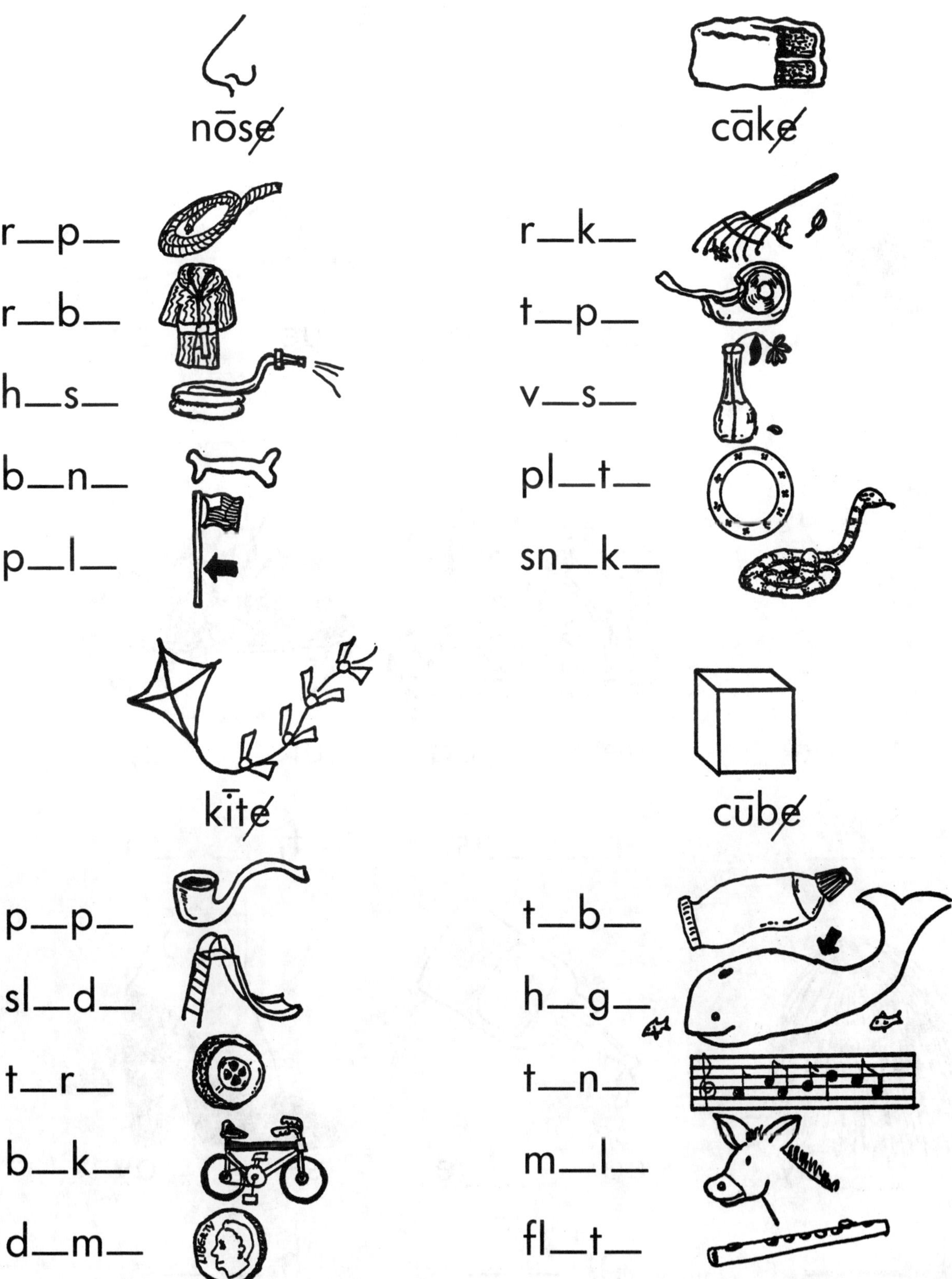

My name is ______________________________.

Circle the vowel letters that complete each word.
Write the vowel letters on the lines.

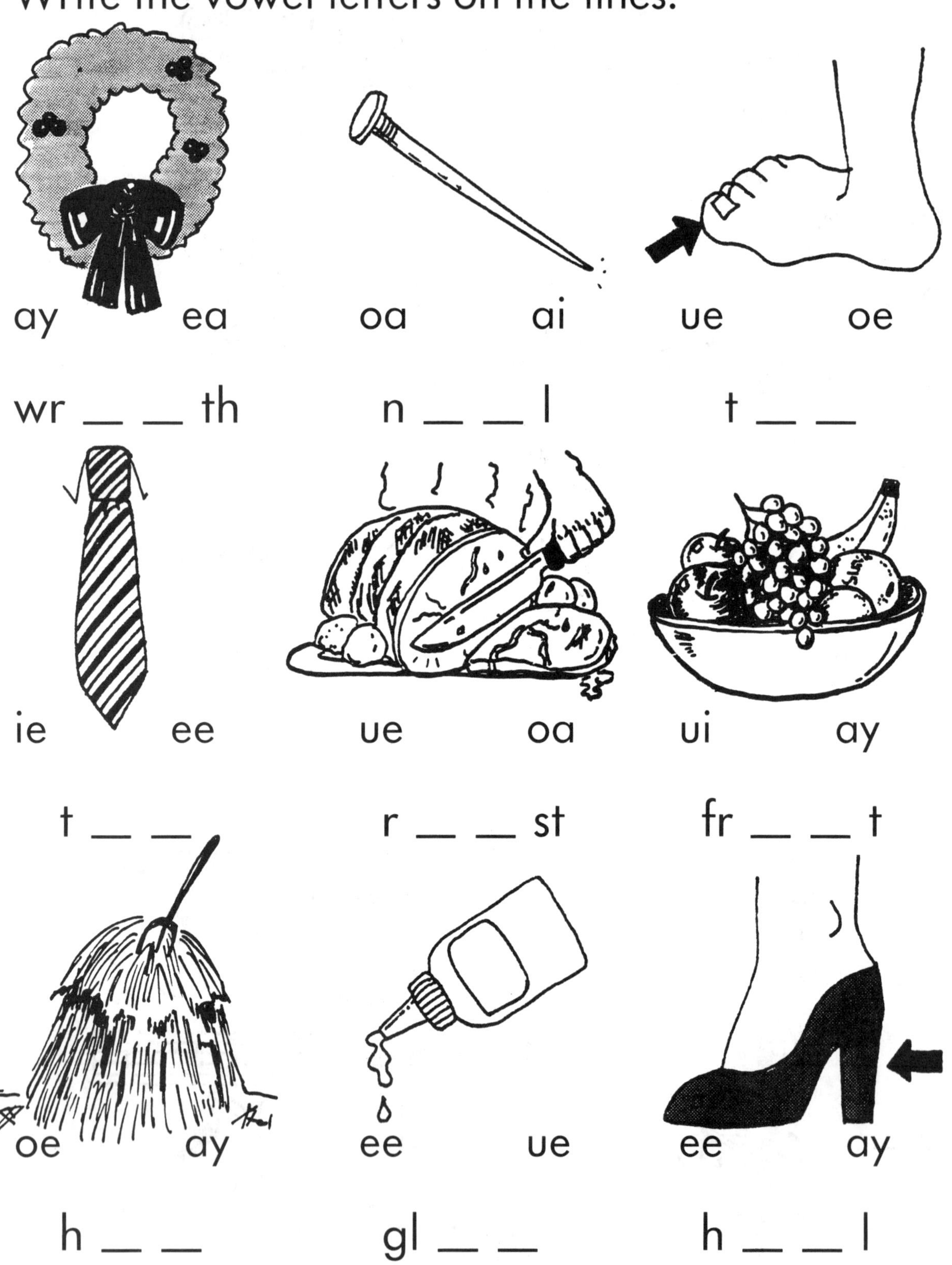

My name is ______________________________.

Write **i** or **e** in the box after each word.

I say i

I say e

pretty	☐	study	☐
cry	☐	monkey	☐
July	☐	sly	☐
fifty	☐	story	☐
copy	☐	library	☐
try	☐	cherry	☐

dry ☐

very ☐

easy ☐

good-bye ☐

lucky ☐

My name is ______________________________.

Do you know the secret message?
Write the vowel letter of the picture on the line.
Then write the letter in the numbered box.
Read the message.

1.  ____ 2.  ____ 3. 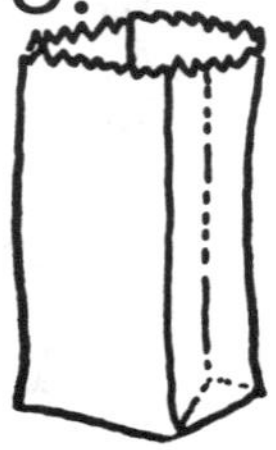 ____ 4.  ____ 5.  ____ 6.  ____ 7. ____

8.  ____ 9.  ____ 10.  ____ 11.  ____ 12.  ____ 13.  ____ 14. ____

V[1.]w[2.]ls h[3.]v[4.] m[5.]ny s[6.][7.]nds.

[8.] kn[9.]w th[10.] v[11.]w[12.]l s[13.][14.]nds.

My name is ________________________________.

Fill in the missing letters to complete the puzzle. The words have a short vowel sound.

1. a very little bug

2. bread for a hot dog

3. a stone

4. laid by a bird

5. sick

6. an airplane

7. a number less than 10

8. a tool

9. wet dirt

10. a kind of meat

1.		n		
2.	b			
3.			c	
4.			g	
5.		l		
6.	j			
7.	s			
8.		x		
9.			d	
10.	h			

My name is ____.

Fill in the missing letters to complete the puzzle. The words have a long vowel sound.

1. a short, funny story
2. a girl or woman
3. real
4. hello
5. a body of water
6. ten cents
7. a law
8. at no cost
9. a bucket
10. a flower

1.			k	
2.	s			
3.		r		e
4.	h			
5.	l			
6.			m	e
7.	r			
8.				e
9.			i	
10.			s	

My name is ___________________________________.

Write the words that have a long **i** sound on a cloud in the sky. Write the words that have a long **e** sound on a cherry.

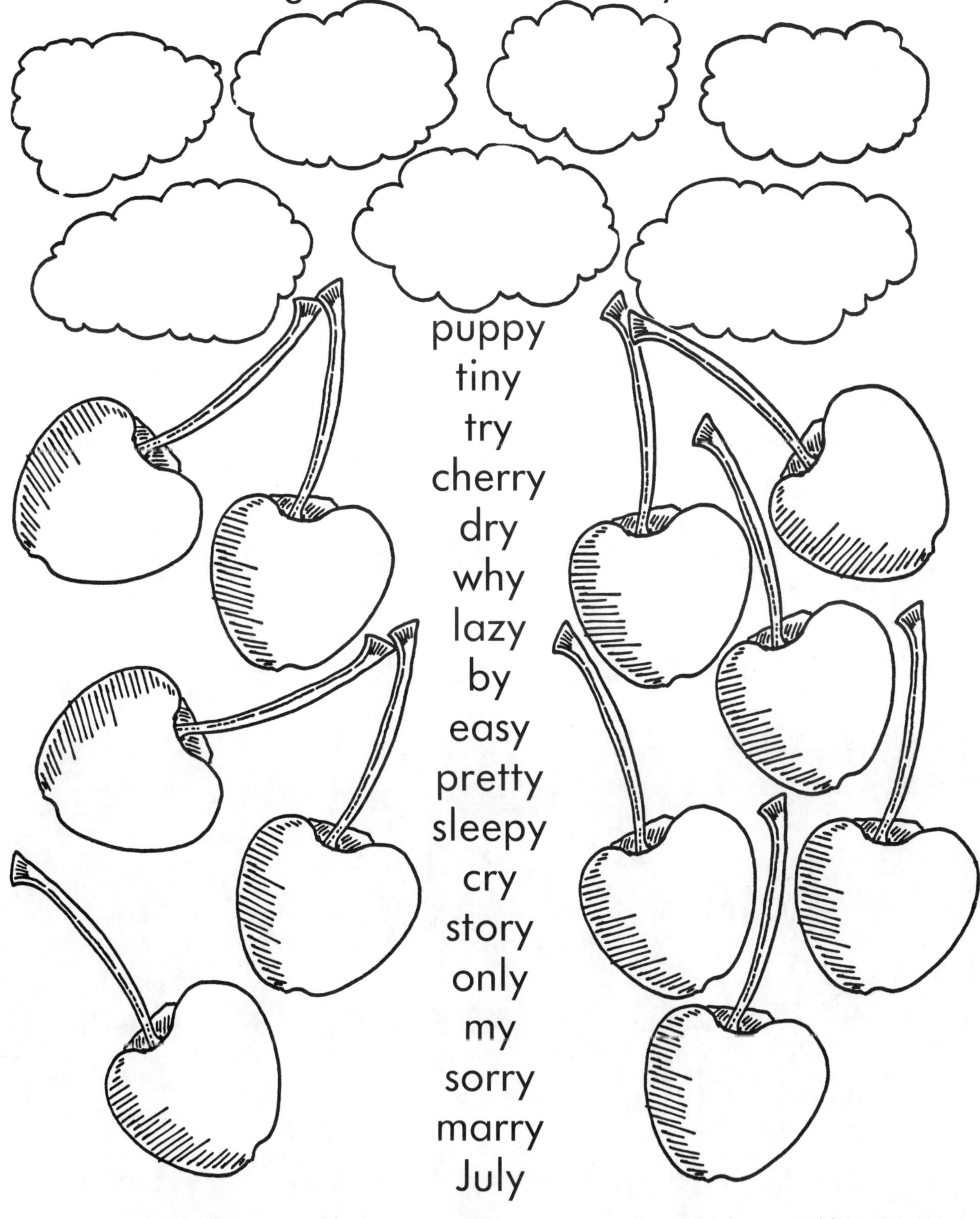

Dear Parent or Guardian:

We have just completed the third unit of *Phonics in Context* in the program *INSIGHTS: Reading as Thinking*. This unit reviews long and short vowel sounds in one-syllable words. We also compared words with long and short vowel sounds such as cute and cut. We used the following four generalizations about vowel sounds:

1. When a word has one vowel letter at the beginning or in the middle, usually the word has a short vowel sound.
   EXAMPLE: **pen**

2. When a word has only one vowel letter, and it is at the end of the word, usually the vowel has a long sound.
   EXAMPLE: **be, go,** and **she**

3. When a word has two vowels and one is a final **e**, usually the first vowel says its name and the final **e** is silent.
   EXAMPLE: **nice**

4. When two vowel letters are together in a word, usually the first vowel says its name and the second vowel is silent.
   EXAMPLE: **bean**

To help your child connect phonic skills to meaningful stories you can make your own books at home. Staple together a few sheets of paper to make a blank book. Ask your child to recount a family event or story. Help your child write the words on the left-hand pages or at the bottom of each page. Keep the focus on the meaning or sense of the story and don't insist on correct spelling when your child spells a big word the way it sounds. Do, however, remind your child that the four phonic rules given above can be as useful when writing as when reading. After your child has created the artwork, you will have a family keepsake, and your child's creativity and language skills can be celebrated.

Sincerely,

Your Child's Teacher

Literature List

Cannon, Jannell. *Stellaluna.* Harcourt, 1993. A delightful story of a lost baby bat who tries to grow up with a nest of birds.

Cooney, Barbara. *Hattie and the Wild Waves.* Viking, 1990. A daughter of German-American immigrants in turn-of-the century Brooklyn is determined to become a painter.

De Paola, Tomie. *The Mysterious Giant of Barletta: an Italian Folktale.* Harcourt, 1984. The town's giant statue comes to life and, using a clever trick, stops an outside army from invading his peaceful village.

Jeffers, Susan. *Brother Eagle, Sister Sky.* Dial, 1991. A speech given by Chief Seattle over one hundred years ago sensitively conveys a reverence for nature.

Johnson, Angela. *Do Like Kyla.* Watts, 1990. Kyla turns the tables on her little sister who loves to imitate.

Pfister, Marcus. *The Rainbow Fish.* North-South, 1992. An award-winning story of a lonely fish who learns to make friends.

Waber, Bernard. *Ira Says Goodbye.* Houghton Mifflin, 1988. When Ira finds out that his best friend Reggie is moving away, he has to learn how to deal with the situation.

Wood, Douglas. *Old Turtle.* Pfeifer-Hamilton, 1992. This book won several awards for its sensitive view of the nature of God.

Yolen, Jane. *The Ballad of Pirate Queens.* Harcourt, 1995. The story of two famous female pirates, Anne Bonney and Mary Reade.

Zemach, Margot. *The Three Wishes: an Old Story.* Farrar, 1986. A woodcutter and his wife are granted wishes when they help an imp who is caught under a fallen tree.

My name is ______________________________.

Write the correct consonant blend under each picture.

scr spr shr

My name is ________________________________.

Circle the word you hear in each row.

1.	scare	scream	shrine	seam
2.	spray	play	spot	shred
3.	scold	screech	spree	teach
4.	shriek	sheet	seek	screen
5.	shell	shrill	scroll	sill
6.	spree	tree	speak	scream
7.	shred	said	shed	spread
8.	rain	Spain	screen	sprain
9.	scale	patch	scratch	shift
10.	shrug	bug	plug	smog

My name is ________________________________.

Read each sentence.
Decide which word best completes the sentence.
Circle that word.
Write the three-letter consonant blend
on the line to complete the word.

scr	spr	shr

1. My little sister uses crayons to ________ibble on the walls.

   scribble spribble shribble

2. Your sweater may ________ink if you wash it in hot water.

   scrink sprink shrink

3. George will ________ub the floor with soap and water.

   scrub sprub shrub

4. My fingers ____ivel____ up if I leave them in the water too long.

scrivel   sprivel   shrivel

5. I always have ____ambled____ eggs for breakfast.

scrambled   sprambled   shrambled

6. We put the ____eds____ of paper in the rabbit's cage.

screds   spreds   shreds

7. The flowers begin to grow in ____ing____.

scring   spring   shring

8. I ____aped____ all the paint off my lunchbox.

scraped   spraped   shraped

My name is ______________________________.

Listen as your teacher names each picture. Write the consonant blend you hear under each picture.

str spl thr

My name is ______________________________.

Circle the word you hear in each row.

1.	strain	sane	stain	train
2.	tree	street	three	tea
3.	time	throb	splotch	thumb
4.	spit	sit	split	strict
5.	stick	set	threat	stretch
6.	suck	struck	truck	stuck
7.	smash	sash	splash	trash

My name is ______________________________.

8. thrill	spill	hill	shrill
9. seek	stick	shriek	strike
10. this	thrice	strict	rice
11. blotch	sock	splotch	spot
12. threw	two	stew	scrape
13. sing	string	spring	sting
14. splatter	patter	scrabble	bladder
15. song	strong	throng	wrong

My name is ______________________________.

Read each sentence.
Decide what word best completes the sentence.
Circle that word.
Write the three-letter consonant blend
to complete the word.

str	spl	thr

1. The skunk has a white ________ipe on its back.

   stripe splipe thripe

2. My cat loves to play with a ball of ________ing .

   string spling thring

3. I drank hot soup for my sore ________oat .

   stroat sploat throat

4. Please do not ________ow away your soda bottle.

   strow splow throw

My name is ____.

5. I had a wonderful banana ______it for dessert.

strit split thrit

6. Ducks like to __________ash in a pond.

strash splash thrash

7. Bears are very __________ong animals.

strong splong throng

8. The monster in the movie looked very

__________ange .

strange splange thrange

9. Carlos needed blue __________ead to sew the button on his shirt.

stread splead thread

10. If you are not careful with your brush, you may

__________atter the paint.

stratter splatter thratter

My name is ____.

Read each sentence.
Decide which word best completes the sentence.
Circle that word.
Write the three-letter consonant blend
to complete the word.

scr	str	thr

1. Randy ___________ew the baseball to the player on first base.

   screw strew threw

2. The ___________ap on my shoe suddenly broke.

   scrap strap thrap

3. The children will ___________eam as they watch the monster movie!

   scream stream thream

4. King George sat upon his ___________one in the land of Nod.

   scrone strone throne

My name is ______________________________.

Use the blends below for the next group of sentences.

spr	spl	shr

5. I always order fried ____________imp when we eat at the fish restaurant.

sprimp splimp shrimp

6. The little plant began to ____________out a few days after I watered it.

sprout splout shrout

7. I got a ____________inter in my toe from running on the wood floor.

sprinter splinter shrinter

8. Many plants begin to grow in the season called ____________ing .

spring spling shring

My name is ______________________________.

Read each sentence.
Decide which word best completes the sentence.
Circle that word. Write it on the line.

1. I use a ruler to draw __________ lines on my paper.

   street straight struck

2. My pants were too big. I washed them in hot water so they would __________ .

   shrink shrimp shred

3. I __________ my sandwich in half and shared it with a friend.

   splash split splatter

4. Paula likes to __________ peanut butter on her toast.

   spring spread spray

5. If you get __________ strikes in baseball, you are out.

   thread throat three

My name is ______________________________.

Read each sentence.
Decide which word best completes the sentence.
Write the three-letter consonant blend
that completes the word in the sentence.

thr	str	shr

1. In our backyard there are some tall trees and one little ________ub.

   thrub strub shrub

2. A zebra is an animal with black ________ipes.

   thripes stripes shripes

3. I bought a needle and ________ead to sew my shirt.

   thread stread shread

4. I helped my little sister walk across the ________eet.

   threet street shreet

My name is ____________________________________.

Use the blends below for the next group of sentences.

spr	spl	scr

5. Every morning I __________ead butter and jelly on my bread.

spread splead scread

6. I like to __________amble my eggs for breakfast.

spramble splamble scramble

7. Rose painted her room for the first time. She __________attered paint all over the floor.

sprattered splattered scrattered

8. Brad had to __________ub the floor for a long time.

sprub splub scrub

My name is ______________________________.

Read each sentence.
Decide which word best completes the sentence.
Write it on the line.

1. The farmer wore a yellow hat made of ________ .

strain straw stray

2. We crawled ____________ the dark tunnel to get to the other side.

three through throat

3. I gave my baby brother a pencil and a piece of paper to ____________ on.

scream scribble scrub

4. This sweater may ____________ if I put it in the dryer.

shrimp shrink shrub

5. Mr. Green will __________ the plants with water.

spread spring spray

My name is ____.

Read each question. Write the answer on the line.

1. Would you sprow or throw a ball?

   I would ____________________ a ball.

2. Do ducks splash or strash in water?

   Ducks ____________________ in water.

3. Do flowers bloom in the shring or the spring?

   Flowers bloom in the ____________________ .

4. Would you thramble or scramble your eggs for breakfast?

   I would ____________________ my eggs for breakfast.

5. A sweater might shrink or splink in a washing machine?

   A sweater might ____________________ in a washing machine.

My name is ______________________________.

Read each question. Write the answer on the line.

6. Does a zebra have many stripes or scripes?

A zebra has many ____________________ .

7. Would you scrub or splub the floor?

I would ____________________ the floor.

8. Do you see cars on the threet or the street?

I see cars on the ____________________ .

9. Do you sew with a needle and thread or splead?

I sew with a needle and ____________________ .

10. Do you spread or scread peanut butter on toast?

I ____________________ peanut butter on toast.

My name is ____.

Read the story below.
Decide what words are missing from the story.
Choose words from the box to complete the story.
Write the missing words in the blanks.
Draw a picture in the space at the bottom of each page to illustrate each part of the story.

screen	shriek	street	shrubs
stretched	scratched	thrilling	
throbbing	sprayed	splattered	

My kitten, Sprite, was outside having a good time running down the ________________ . She sniffed the flowers and pranced around the ________________ on people's lawns.

My name is ____.

Suddenly, someone ________________ her with a water hose. Sprite was so frightened that she let out a loud ________________ and scurried away. She quickly ran home and ________________ the door with her claws.

I opened the ________________ door and saw my poor little kitten shivering on the porch.

My name is ______________________________.

"Oh, Sprite," I cried, "you are soaking wet!" She shook her dripping body and ______________ water all over the floor. I got a big towel from the closet to wipe off the water. I could feel Sprite's heart ______________ as I dried her fur. She ______________ out on the rug and began to purr. I have a feeling Sprite was very happy to be home. It had not been a ______________ day for her.

Dear Parent or Guardian:

We have just completed the fourth unit of *Phonics in Context* in the program *INSIGHTS: Reading as Thinking*. In this unit we studied six three-letter blends:

scr as in **screen**
spr as in **spray**
shr as in **shrimp**
str as in **strawberry**
spl as in **splash**
thr as in **throw**

You can help your child apply his or her knowledge of three-letter blends by playing a game with alphabet cereal. Pour out a bowl of letters for each of you. Say a word with a three-letter blend and ask your child to spell it using the cereal. Ask your child to name three-letter blend words for you to spell with the cereal letters. Eating the words, of course, means the end of the game.

When you read aloud any of the books listed on the back of this page, ask your child to read the last word in each line of type. Your child can be the "End Word Wizard." This changes listening to a story into a participatory event. As your child's reading becomes more and more fluid, you might ask him or her to read every other line of type or every other page. Encourage the use of special voices for characters, sound effects, or other ways to make the story come alive. After reading, your child might like to make paper bag puppets of the main characters and use them to help retell or act out the story.

Sincerely,

Your Child's Teacher

Literature List

Adoff, Arnold. *Street Music.* HaperCollins, 1995. A poetic look at people, parks, buildings, and problems of city life.

Cole, Joanna. *The Magic Schoolbus Inside the Earth.* Scholastic, 1990. With a teacher like Mrs. Frizzle, anything can happen and a great deal does.

Day, Alexandra. *Carl Makes a Scrapbook.* Farrar, 1994. Carl the dog and his human friend create a wonderful book by pasting pictures in a scrapbook.

Johnson, Angela. *One of Three.* Orchard, 1995. The youngest of three children tells about school, shopping, and riding the subway with her older sisters.

Kroll, Virginia L. *Naomi Knows It's Springtime.* Caroline House, 1993. A sensory story of the beginning of spring has a surprise ending.

Trivizas, Eugene. *The Three Little Wolves and the Big Bad Pig.* McElderry, 1993. In a clever switch on the familiar story, the pig wrecks each structure the wolves build until the surprise harmonious ending.

Viorst, Judith. *My Mama Says There Aren't Any Zombies, Ghosts, Vampires, Creatures, Demons, Monsters, Fiends, Goblins, or Things.* Atheneum, 1973. Nick tries to sleep in spite of the unsettling noises. He is worried that mamas aren't always right.

Williams, Vera B. *Stringbean's Trip to the Shining Sea.* Scholastic, 1988. Stringbean's West Coast adventures are told on postcards he sends to the reader.

Wittman, Patricia. *Scrabble Creek.* Macmillan, 1993. A young girl conquers her fears when she has to walk in the dark to the bunkhouse to go to sleep. Written in first person, the story deals with the fear of the dark that is so common.

My name is ______________________________.

Part 1: Circle the word that names the picture.

Part 2: Circle the word with the **oi** or **oy** sound.
Color the matching box.

coin cook cake	toy town tail	noise nose nurse	ball boil bold
oi | oy	oi | oy	oi | oy	oi | oy
boy bay boat	oil old owl	jay jar joy	sell soil sale
oi | oy	oi | oy	oi | oy	oi | oy

My name is ____________________________________.

Write a word from the box to complete each sentence.

1. We will ____________ hamburgers for dinner.

2. I broke the ____________ on my pencil.

3. The food won't ____________ in the freezer.

4. ____________ has a tree house in his backyard.

5. The ship went on a long ____________ .

6. I ____________ swimming in the summer.

7. Chris may ____________ the Girl Scouts.

8. Cecil will buy a ____________ for his baby sister.

Roy	broil	voyage
oil	enjoy	spoil
point	toy	join

My name is ______________________________________.

Write a word from the box to complete each sentence.

1. I like to drink milk with a __________ .

2. The man will __________ away the dirt in his truck.

3. School was closed __________ of a holiday.

4. The __________ is a kind of bird.

5. The baby __________ on the floor.

6. I __________ a cold last winter.

7. The bear's __________ are long and sharp.

8. We had a picnic lunch on the __________ .

hawk	lawn	claws
taught	straw	because
haul	caught	crawls

My name is ______________________________.

Write a word from the box to complete each sentence.

1. Lynn took her dog for a __________ .

2. I like __________ and pepper on my eggs.

3. Cover your mouth when you __________ .

4. The teacher uses __________ to write on the board.

5. The __________ man has no hair.

6. I __________ a plant for my mother.

7. Tom will __________ me on the phone.

8. A baby is a __________ person.

cough	bald	call
small	walk	bought
chalk	salt	thought

My name is ________________________________.

Fill in the missing letters.

raw	ball
cough	salt
auto	daughter
draw	paws

1. Another name for a car is __ __to.
2. Dogs walk on their p__ __s.
3. I put s__ __t on my food.
4. When you have a cold you c__ __gh.
5. A food that is uncooked is r__ __.
6. We dr__ __ pictures with crayons.
7. A little girl is her parents' d__ __ghter.
8. A b__ __l is a toy you can bounce.

My name is ________________________________.

Circle the word that names the picture.

My name is ________________________________.

Part 1: Circle the word that names the picture.

Part 2: Write an X next to each word in which **ow** has the long **o** sound.

____ cow	____ down	____ own
____ low	____ frown	____ flow
____ know	____ slow	____ gown
____ how	____ grow	____ row
____ show	____ power	____ throw

My name is ______________________________.

Find the answer to each riddle.
Write it on the line.

glows	plows
mow	flows
crow	brown
town	blow

1. It is another name for city. ________________

2. It is something a candle does. ________________

3. It is a bird that is black. ________________

4. It is a color. ________________

5. It is something we do to grass. ________________

6. It is something a farmer does to a field.

   ____

7. It is something you do to make bubbles.

   ____

8. It is something a river does. ________________

My name is ____.

Part 1: Circle the word that names the picture.

Part 2: Circle the word that makes sense in the sentence.

1. My (cousin, count) came to visit me.

2. Sue has (flour, four) sisters.

3. I can (pour, pout) my own milk.

4. The sand felt (rough, round) on my feet.

5. I like to (touch, about) things in a store.

My name is ______________________________________.

Write the word that names the picture.

bow	trouble	cow	pour
four	crown	clown	crow
cloud	touch	house	bowl

My name is ______________________________.

Write the word that names the picture.

book	foot	rooster	moose
hood	moon	poodle	broom
wood	spoon	pool	boot

My name is ______________________________.

Part 1: Circle the word that names the picture.

Part 2: Circle the word that has the same sound as new or rule. Color the matching box.

flew fly float		turn tune team		rude ride run		now new not	
ew	u	ew	u	ew	u	ew	u
growl grow grew		jar June joy		blew black blow		July joke just	
ew	u	ew	u	ew	u	ew	u

My name is ____.

Circle the word that makes sense in each sentence.

1. A plane (flew, flow) over my house.

2. I pulled out my (two, tooth) last night.

3. We use a (rub, ruler) in class.

4. I heard a bird sing a happy (tube, tune).

5. We had a play at my (school, soon).

6. Tim reads a lot of (boats, books).

7. Liz has a (hide, hood) on her coat.

8. I (threw, three) the ball to Ann.

9. We swim in a (pull, pool).

10. I have a (now, new) pair of shoes.

My name is ______________________________.

Circle the word you hear.

1. coin, cow, coat	2. slow, sand, saw	3. cool, chew, choke
4. stir, stall, stick	5. born, barn, bone	6. all, oil, owl
7. thought, throat, thorn	8. farm, fern, flow	9. curl, call, car
	10. farm, four, fall	

Cut out the words.

toy	draw	cow
crow	trouble	four
moon	star	corn
round	bird	look

My name is ______________________.

Circle the vowel sound you hear.
Color the matching box.

My name is ______________________________.

Write the word that names the picture.

snow	crow	fountain	mouth
trouble	house	country	crown
flower	clown	pour	four

My name is ______________________________.

Color the rhyming pairs any color you like.
Color the pairs that do not rhyme blue.

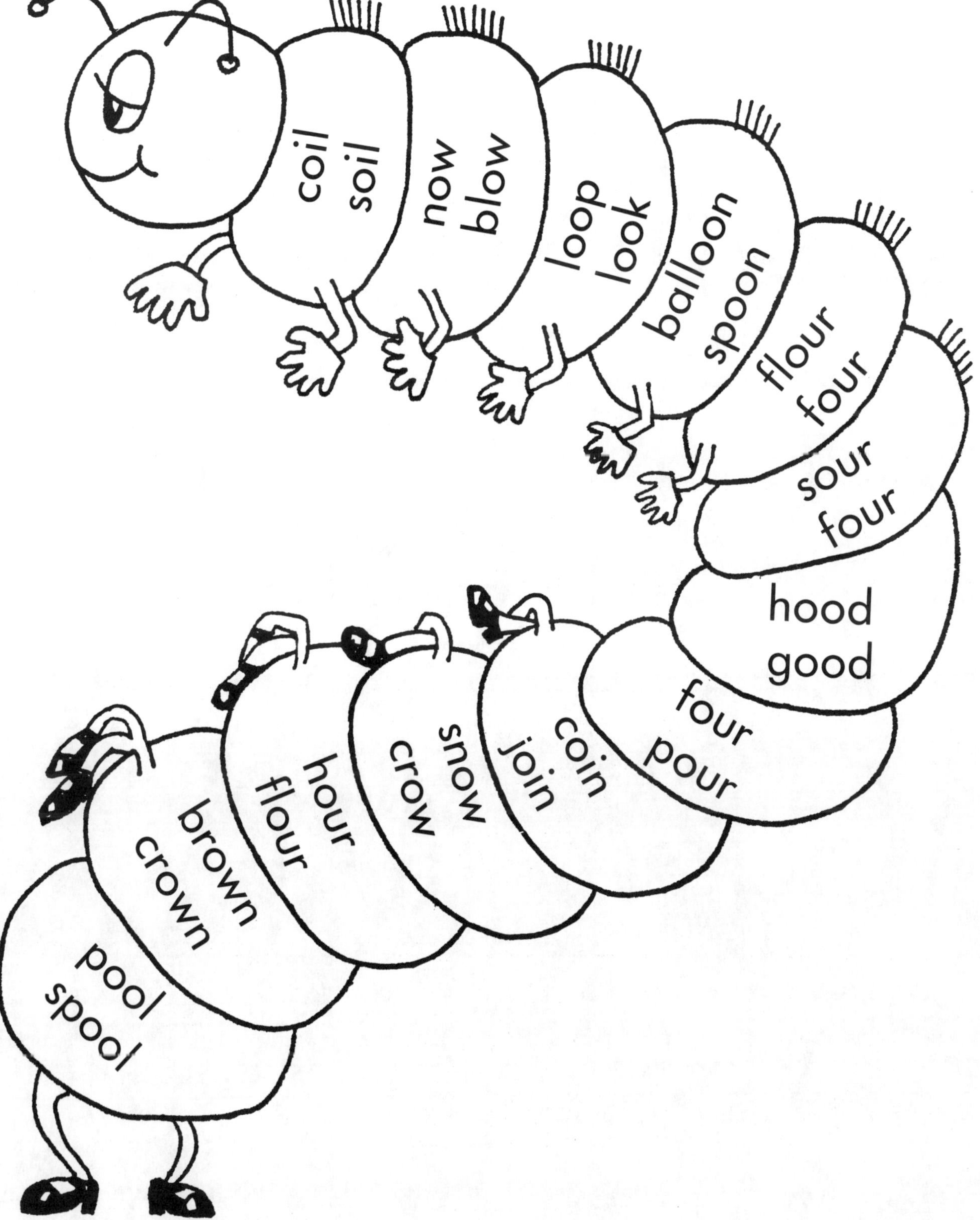

Dear Parent or Guardian:

We have just completed the fifth unit of *Phonics in Context* in the program *INSIGHTS: Reading as Thinking.* In this unit we studied the special vowel sounds of **a, o,** and **u** represented by the following letter combinations:

oi as in **boil**
oy as in **boy**
aw as in **saw**

au as in **auto**
al as in **walk**

ou as in **couch**
ow as in **cow**

oo as in **moon**
ew as in **new**
u as in **rule**

The books listed on the back of this letter provide many opportunities to read words with these vowel sounds. They are also great stories. To help your child see the importance of reading in everyday situations, make grocery shopping into a shared responsibility. Your child could write the shopping list, read the ads in the supermarket circulars or Sunday newspaper, cut out and sort coupons, or read labels and signs in the grocery store. These stages of planning and shopping provide you with opportunities to reinforce the reading skills that relate to numbers and math.

Sincerely,

Your Child's Teacher

Literature List

Allard, Harry. *I Will Not Go to Market Today.* Dial, 1981. A rooster keeps getting delayed on the way to the store.

Fox, Mem. *Tough Boris.* Harcourt, 1994. Boris von der Borch is a mean, greedy, old pirate, but he loves his pet.

Galdone, Paul. *Puss in Boots.* Clarion, 1979. After the miller dies, his youngest son gets only his quick-witted cat. See how the cat helps him marry the princess.

Kilroy, Sally. *Market Day.* Viking, 1986. Compare this book to your own shopping trips.

McCloskey, Robert. *Make Way for Ducklings.* Puffin, 1969. A Caldecott Award winner, this is the endearing story of the mallards who raise their ducklings in a city full of surprises.

McKissack, Patricia. *A Million Fish.* Knopf, 1992. A tall tale about catching and losing fish, with lots of number fun.

Morris, Winifred. *What if the Shark Wears Tennis Shoes?* Atheneum, 1990. Stephen's greatest nighttime fear is that a shark will get all the way upstairs and into his room while he is sleeping.

Ray, Mary Lyn. *Pumpkins.* Harcourt, 1992. A man grows and sells his crop of pumpkins and rescues what he loves.

Ryder, Joanne. *A House by the Sea.* Morrow, 1994. A boy thinks about living where he could play with seals, crabs, a whale, and an octopus.

Yolen, Jane. *Owl Moon.* Philomel, 1987. Caldecott Medal. Spend a magical moonlit winter's night calling for owls with a father and child.

My name is ____________________________________.

Circle the word that names the picture.

My name is ______________________________.

Circle the word that names the picture.
Color the matching box.

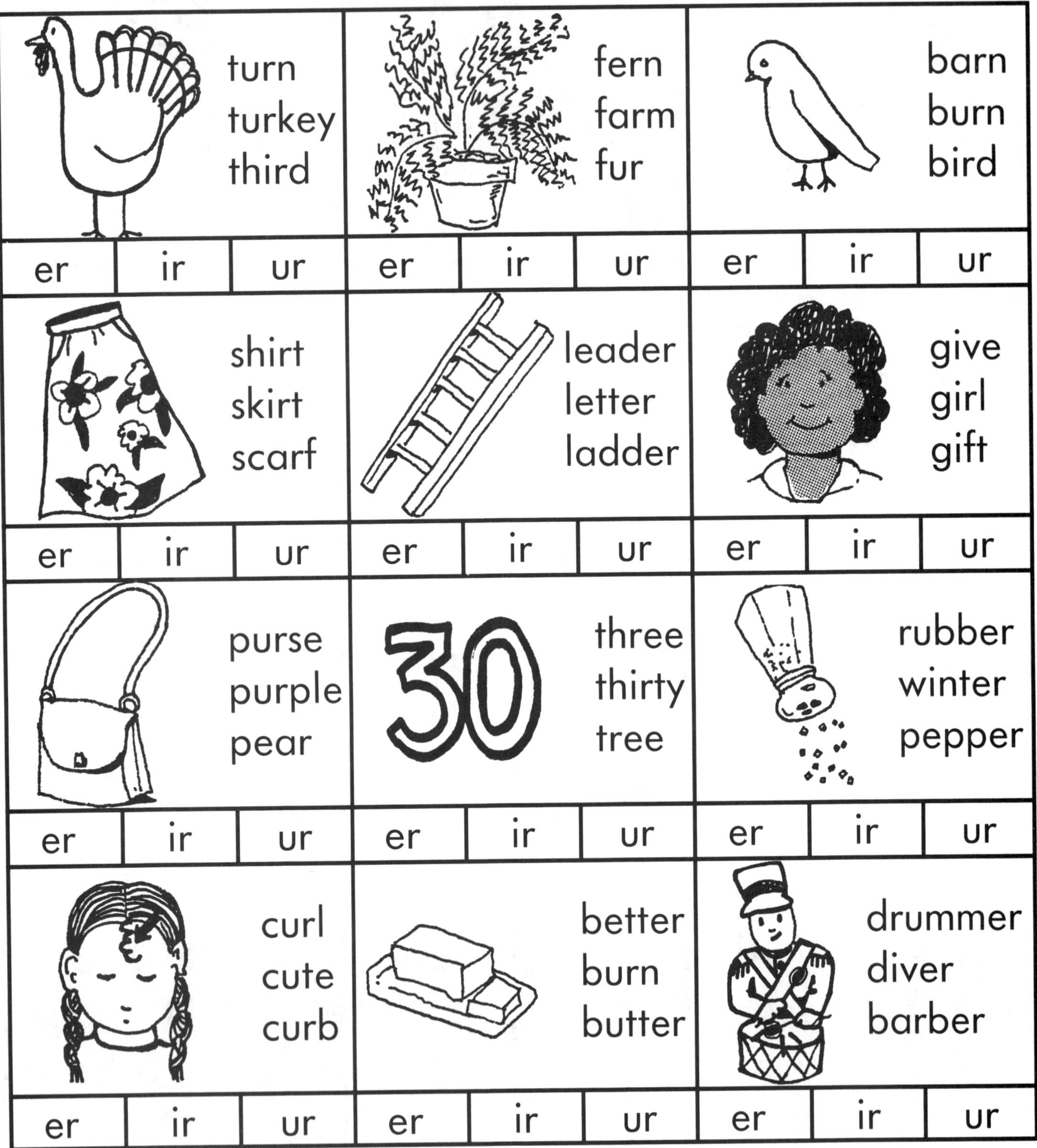

My name is ____________________________________.

Circle the words that match the sound shown by the letters in each box.

ir — fork, skirt, shirt, girl	**ur** — purse, cord, church, chart	**er** — letter, clerk, fort, hammer
ur — burn, barn, hurt, fort	**ir** — bird, first, fork, farm	**er** — farmer, spider, summer, garden
ir — third, thorn, three, thirty	**ur** — fur, far, curb, star	**ir** — stir, store, farm, chirp

My name is ______________________________.

Listen to the word that names the picture.
Circle the special vowel sound you hear.

My name is ______________________________.

Write the word that names the picture.

ruler	card	car	jar
bird	arm	hurt	third
yard	turkey	cart	fort

My name is ______________________________.

Circle the word you hear.

1.	2.	3.
warm wall well	touch third throw	joke jar joy
4.	**5.**	**6.**
told tore toad	tune torch turn	rubber ruling really
7.	**8.**	**9.**
horse house hold	bright brown barn	moon more money
	10.	
	pause part port	

Cut out the words.

card	fern	arm
yard	third	four
burn	star	corn
for	bird	church

My name is ____________________________________.

Color the rhyming pairs any color you like.
Color the pairs that do not rhyme blue.

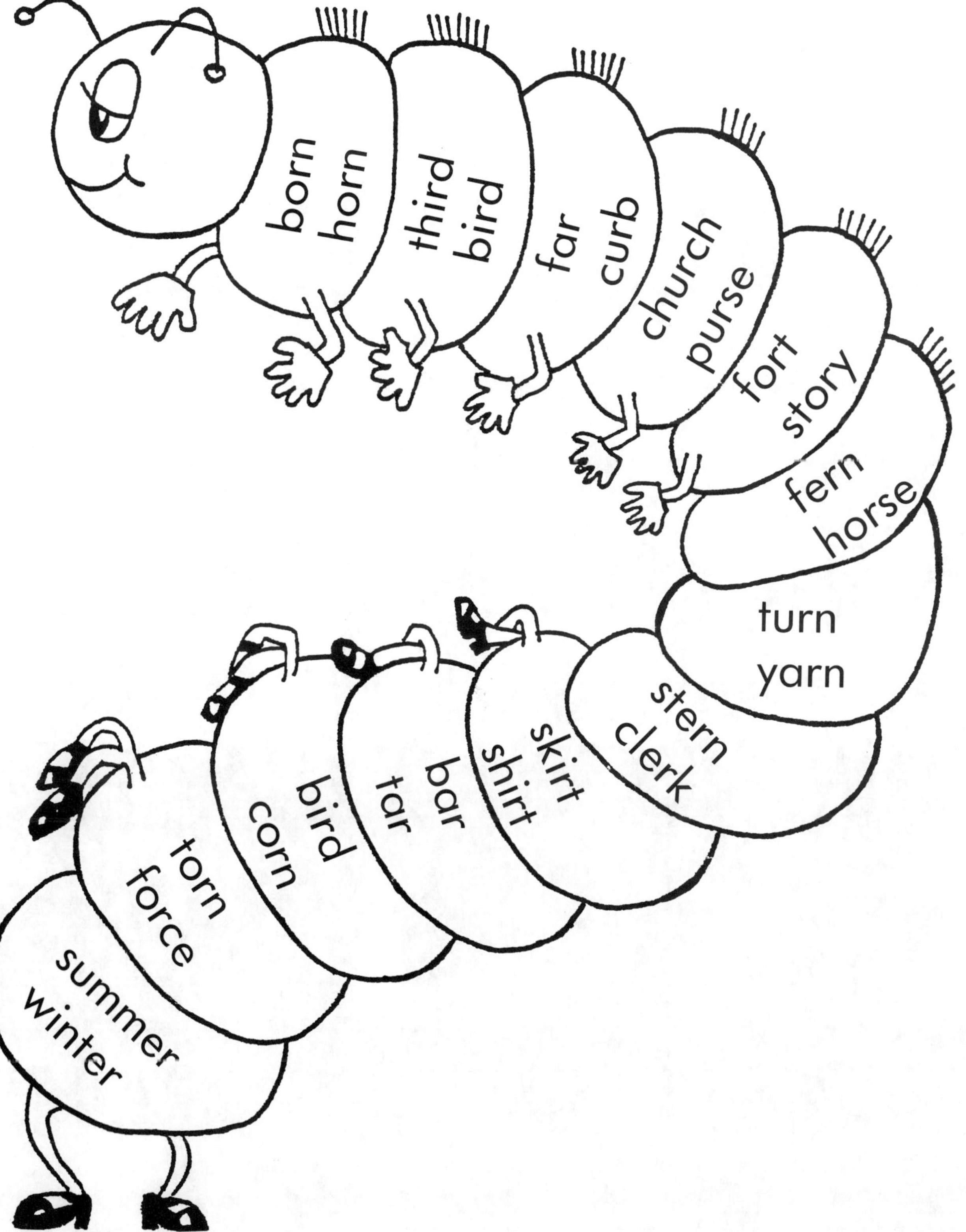

Dear Parent or Guardian:

We have just completed the sixth unit of *Phonics in Context* in the program *INSIGHTS: Reading as Thinking.* In this unit we studied the following r-controlled vowel sounds:

ar as in **car**
er as in **fern**
ir as in **bird**
ur as in **nurse**
or as in **corn**

It's important to read to your child whenever you can, but for a change of pace, have your child read to you. Even though the reading may be less than perfect, you can both enjoy the characters and plot of the story. Among other benefits, by reading a story to you, your child learns to see himself or herself as a reader.

After reading one of the stories listed on the back of this letter, ask your child what part of the book he or she liked best, or what else the child knows or imagines in relation to the main characters or the topic of the book. Look at the illustrations again and ask your child to choose the one he or she likes the best. If the illustrations stimulate new ideas, your child may want to create his or her own pictures.

Sincerely,

Your Child's Teacher

Literature List

Boelts, Maribeth. *Grace and Joe.* Whitman, 1994. A quiet story of two friends, one of whom is a mail carrier.

Brown, Marc. *Arthur's First Sleepover.* Little, 1994. One of a series, this good-humored story is about sleeping in a back-yard tent.

Brown, Margaret Wise. *Four Fur Feet.* Hyperion, 1994. A rhyming story of familiar animal sounds and one mysterious animal with silent furry feet.

Freeman, Don. *Corduroy.* Puffin, 1968. A bear loses a button, but finds a friend.

Kroll, Virginia. *New Friends, True Friends, Stuck-Like-Glue Friends.* Eerdmans, 1994. A cheerful catalog of friendship in all its appealing forms.

O'Hearn, Michael. *Hercules the Harbor Tug.* Charlesbridge, 1995. Two children go out on a tug and see oil spills, dredgers, ships, lighthouses, dry docks, and marine wildlife.

Prelutsky, Jack. *The Dragons are Singing Tonight.* Greenwillow, 1993. Seventeen incredible poems to amuse and amaze dragon fans.

Seuss, Dr. *Yertle the Turtle and Other Stories.* Random House, 1958. Three modern fables have improbable characters and appropriate moral lessons.

Sharmat, Mitchell. *Gregory, the Terrible Eater.* Scholastic, 1980. Gregory, a goat, refuses to eat the delicious tin cans, old clothes, and bottle caps his parents provide.

My name is ______________________________________.

Complete each sentence with a word from the box.

write	wrong	wrist	wrap	wreck

1. Father turned the ____________________ way at the second corner and got lost.

2. I will ____________________ up grandmother's birthday present in this red and yellow striped paper.

3. People stopped on the road to look at the

   ____________________ .

4. Joan wears a watch on her left ________________ .

5. My five-year-old sister is beginning to

   ____________________ her name.

My name is ______________________________________.

Complete each sentence with a word from the box.

knock	know	knew	knife	knight

1. I didn't ____________________ that I had your jacket.

2. Be careful with the ____________________ when you cut your sandwich.

3. Once I read a story about a brave

   ____________________ .

4. Jack ____________________ the answer to the first question, so he raised his hand.

5. He didn't have to ____________________ on the door to the old house because the door opened by itself.

My name is ____.

Circle the words with the silent letter **k** and silent letter **w**. Write the words on the lines below each sentence.

1. Willy Knight wondered what was wrong. Someone was knocking loudly at the back door.

_______________ _______________ _______________

2. Willy's mother had written Willy a note. She tied a knot and hung the note on the doorknob.

_______________ _______________ _______________

3. Mom wrote, "Don't wear the pants with the torn knee. Please wrap the presents for the party."

__________ __________ __________

4. Willy knew it was early. He looked at his wristwatch. He heard the knocking at the back door again.

__________ __________ __________

5. Willy wriggled out of bed and rubbed his eyes. He knew the person at the door would have sore knuckles if he didn't hurry.

__________ __________ __________

My name is ______________________________.

Underline the word in each list that has the same silent consonant letter or letters as the first word. Draw a line through the silent consonant letter or letters in both underlined words.

1. nic̸kel
   cook
   coin
   roc̸k

2. dumb
   bump
   climb
   mumble

3. neighbor
   sign
   name
   might

4. match
   pitch
   mat
   tack

5. quack
   quarter
   bake
   chicken

6. catch
   kitchen
   chipmunk
   pick

7. straight
   taken
   stretch
   lightning

8. crumb
   cub
   comb
   monkey

9. watch
   water
   pocket
   hitch

10. luck
    lunch
    package
    club

11. fight
    eight
    field
    thief

12. thumb
    month
    both
    limb

My name is ______________________________.

Write the word that answers each riddle.
Draw a line through the silent letter or letters in the word that you write.

crack	neighbor	straight
nickel	kitchen	crumbs
thumb	lightning	watch
package	match	comb

1. I am used to make your hair look neat. I can be carried in your pocket. I am a ______________.

2. You sometimes see me during a rainstorm. I make the sky bright. I am ______________.

3. Perhaps I am your friend. I live nearby. I am your ______________.

4. I am a coin. You can get five pennies for me. I am a ______________.

5. I am part of your hand. You need me to pick up things more easily. I am your ______________.

My name is ______________________________.

6. I am a room in your house. Meals are prepared here. I am the ____________________.

7. I am something you see on sidewalks. You don't want to see me in a dish. I am a ____________________.

8. We are tiny pieces of bread or crackers. Often we are fed to birds. We are ____________________.

9. I make heat and light. I can be very dangerous. I am a ____________________.

10. I am not bent or curly. A ruler can make a line like me. I am ____________________.

11. I can mean "to look." I am also used to tell time. I am a ____________________.

12. I can be a box or a bag. People take me many places. I am a ____________________.

My name is ______________________________________.

Draw a line through the silent consonant letter in each word.

1. answer	2. bridge	3. could
4. scent	5. autumn	6. whistle
7. calf	8. whose	9. half
10. often	11. ghost	12. two
13. gnaw	14. scissors	15. fasten
16. walk	17. listen	18. talk
19. island	20. science	21. oh
22. would	23. whole	24. scene

My name is ______________________________________.

Write the underlined word with the silent consonant letter on the line. Draw a line through the silent consonant letter in the word. Leave the line blank if the underlined word has no silent consonant letter.

______________ 1. Animals like to gnaw, or bite, on all kinds of things.

______________ 2. Chalk breaks easily.

______________ 3. Oh, no! My cat scratched a hole in the chair.

______________ 4. I always fasten my seat belt in the car.

______________ 5. Autumn is another name for fall.

______________ 6. Did you answer all of the test questions?

______________ 7. Emilio likes to buy whole chickens.

______________ 8. It is always warm on the island.

______________ 9. Sonny brought his lunch to school last Wednesday.

My name is ______________________________________.

Write the word on the line that best completes each sentence.
The word must have a silent consonant letter or letters.

---

1. I was ____________________ when Jack and I got lost in the woods.

   scared frightened climb

---

2. My parents said you should not pull and ____________________ your sweater.

   stretch socks wear

---

3. Most granola bars cost more than a ____________________ .

   quarter light nickel

---

4. Aunt Hattie likes to ____________________ when she sits in front of the TV.

   knit sleep climb

---

5. Try to find the ____________________ before you go down those dark stairs.

   bulb switch block

My name is ______________________________________.

6. Animals are said to be ____________________ because they cannot talk.

dumb hatch wild

---

7. "How much does that big box ________________ ?" asked the man in the post office.

cost weigh check

---

8. A group of red ants came into the house through a tiny ____________________ .

luck hole crack

---

9. I thought Bob ____________________ his ABC's.

said write knew

---

10. When my name was picked for a prize, I was ____________________ .

lucky surprised sigh

---

11. In winter, do you ever throw bread ____________ on the snow for the birds to eat?

seeds crumbs sing

My name is ______________________________.

Write the correctly spelled word on the line.

1. rite	write	high
2. lam	________	knit
3. nee	________	package
4. blok	________	wrong
5. nit	________	wrap
6. pach	________	brick
7. clim	________	scratch
8. rap	________	patch
9. nown	________	comb
10. pakage	________	lamb
11. hi	________	climb
12. scrach	________	knee
13. com	________	block
14. rong	________	known
15. brik	________	write

My name is ______________________________.

Draw a line through the silent consonant letter or letters in each word.
Then write a sentence using the word on the line next to it.

1. check ______________________________
2. knew ______________________________
3. lucky ______________________________
4. headlight ______________________________
5. plumber ______________________________
6. hatchet ______________________________
7. neighbor ______________________________
8. knuckle ______________________________
9. wrong ______________________________
10. tight ______________________________

My name is ________________________________.

Draw a line through the silent consonant letter or letters in each word.

1. trick
2. eight
3. catcher
4. limb
5. knife
6. wrote
7. clock
8. neighbor
9. switch
10. wreath
11. lamb
12. knee
13. wrap
14. patch
15. might
16. package
17. brick
18. knit
19. wrist
20. wrong

My name is ______________________________.

Write the words in the list under the key picture with the same silent consonant letter.

Silent w

____

____

Silent k

____

____

Silent c

____

____

Silent b

____

____

Silent gh

____

____

Silent t

____

____

sigh
bug
ghost
knot
cold
wring
cup
comb
weather
freckle
tip
built
write
twins
lock
kind
kitchen
sign
pitcher
note
fight
cabin
knew
lamb
woman

My name is ______________________________.

Complete the story by writing the word with the silent consonant letter or letters on each line.

The Adventures of Ned and Nelly

Adventure 1 — *Ned at Work*

Ned was walking with a ____________________ .
friend crutch

He had hurt his leg while working in the gold mine.

This is how it happened.

It was dark as ____________________ in the mine.
night mud

Ned took ____________________ steps and tripped
small eight

over a big ____________________ . He tried to
stone rock

____________________ himself but couldn't stop falling.
help catch

My name is ________________________________.

He hurt his ____________________ . He called, "Help,
knee toe

help!" Nelly heard Ned crying and called the

____________________ . Firefighters
teacher firefighters

____________________ save people. The firefighters
always often

took Ned from the mine. When he got out into

the ____________________ , Ned thanked everyone.
sunshine daylight

My name is ____.

Complete the story by writing the word with the silent consonant letter or letters on each line.

The Adventures of Ned and Nelly

Adventure 2 — *More Excitement*

When Ned and Nelly got home from the gold mine, Nelly discovered that she had lost her

____________________ . "Where did you lose it?"
ring watch

Ned asked.

"I do not ____________________ ," she said.
understand know

"I might have lost it in the mine or perhaps I lost it this morning at the store."

My name is ______________________________________.

"Did someone take it?" Ned said.

"No, I ______________________ it was not taken.

know think

I think I'm about to ____________________ a cold, too,"

get catch

Nelly ______________________ .

sighed said

"Go upstairs and ______________________ into bed,"

fall climb

said Ned. "I'll ______________________ the store.

call write

Maybe they found your watch."

Then the phone rang. It was the store calling to say that Nelly's watch had been found. Nelly was ______________________ .

happy delighted

Dear Parent or Guardian:

We have just completed the seventh unit of *Phonics in Context* in the program *INSIGHTS: Reading as Thinking.* In this unit we studied the following silent letters:

k as in **know**
t as in **often** or **whistle**
w as in **wrap**

c as in **rock** or **science**
s as in **island**
b as in **lamb**

g as in **sign**
l as in **calf**
gh as in **light** or **highway**

The books listed on the back of this letter are stories that deal with the types of feelings we may experience at one time or another: fear of the unknown, love, cooperating to reach a goal, looking forward to new adventures, and trying to be true to our inner nature. After reading one of these stories (or one with similar themes) ask your child how he or she would have behaved or felt in a similar situation. Ask your child what in his or her life is similar to the story and what is different. Talking about books is a great way to show your child that you value his or her perceptions.

Sincerely,

Your Child's Teacher

Literature List

Buntins, Eve. *Night of the Gargoyles.* Clarion, 1994. When night falls, the stone gargoyles on a museum's walls awaken to frolic and frighten the unfortunate watchman.

Hoff, Syd. *The Lighthouse Children.* HarperCollins, 1994. The lighthouse keepers move to the city and learn how to be happy there.

Mayer, Mercer. *Whinnie the Lovesick Dragon.* Macmillan, 1986. Whinnie tries desperately to win the affection of Alfred the Knight, which is not an easy task.

McCloskey, Robert. *Time of Wonder.* Viking, 1957. This Caldecott Award Book is a poetic description of a summer on a Maine island that ends with a hurricane.

McKissack, Patricia C. *Flossie and the Fox.* Pied Piper, 1986. Lil' Flossie Finley encounters a figure who claims to be a fox and cleverly continues on her way. This tale is based on a Tennessee folktale.

Nixon, Joan Lowery. *When I Am Eight.* Dial, 1994. A boy daydreams about the successes he expects to achieve.

Steptoe, John. *Mufaro's Beautiful Daughters.* Scholastic, 1993. A moral tale of the true beauty that lies within.

My name is ______________________________.

Circle the letters that complete each word.
Write them on the lines.

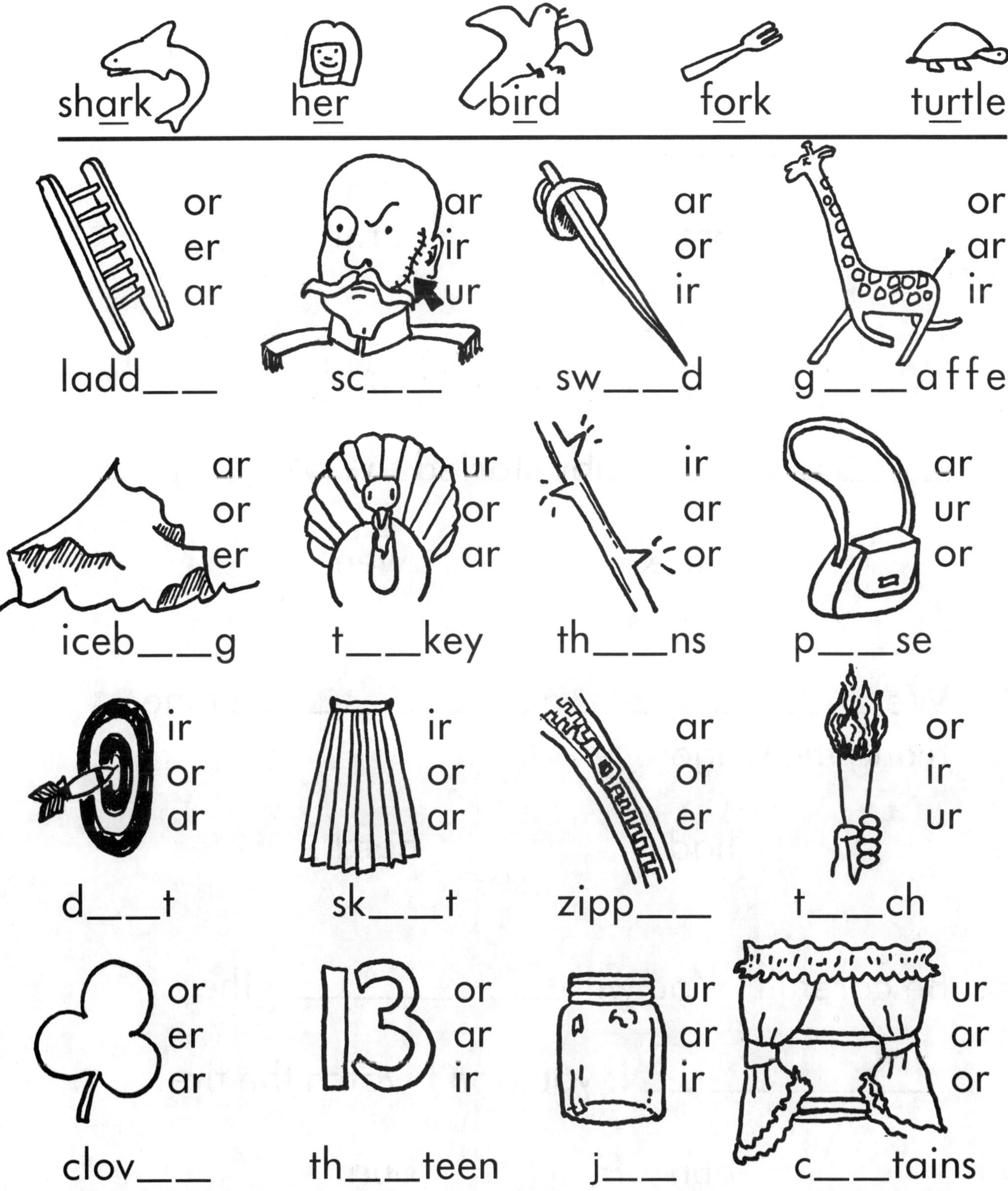

My name is ____.

Fill in each line with the word that best completes the sentence.

1. If I ______________ your friend, don't hurt my

______________ .

am arm

2. Where ______________ you last night when that

______________ baby started to cry?

were wee

3. We ______________ a ______________ time fixing the wagon.

had hard

4. Be careful! You will ______________ the

______________ if you don't watch the fire.

bun burn

My name is ______________________________.

5. We used a ______________ to wash down the ______________ .

hose horse

6. The mouse who lives in the little old ______________ has ______________ his foot.

hut hurt

7. You were the ______________ one to shake your ______________ in the air.

fist first

8. The ______________ and all of the other animals rode to town in the ______________ .

cart cat

9. I wanted to ______________ down the bumpy ______________ of my bed.

pat part

10. ______________ name was something ______________ didn't know.

her he

My name is ________________________________.

Draw a big X on the pictures that have the vowel sounds that you hear in:

auto saw ball

My name is ______________________________.

Decide which word from the list makes sense in each sentence. Write the words on the lines. Use each word only once.

autumn	crawl	small
hall	always	caught
sauce	daughter	paw
straw	awful	salt

1. My baby sister is learning to ______________.
2. Little things are ______________.
3. I like tomato ______________ with my noodles.
4. Taste your food before you put __________ on it.
5. Another name for ______________ is fall.
6. Do you ever drink milk through a ______________?
7. Bill is Mrs. Brown's son and Pam is her ______________.
8. The lion was ______________ in the trap.
9. The students stood quietly in the ______________.
10. I felt ______________ the day I was sick.

My name is ______________________________.

Read the story. The words that have the same vowel sounds as in **book** and **moon** have been underlined. Write the words under the heading Book or Moon on the next page.

No Pool This Time

It was too hot at noon. All of the animals in the woods stood still. Soon the rooster crowed, "Let's go to the brook for a cool drink."

"Good idea," honked the goose.

"I'll bring some food," said the kangaroo.

The horse looked and saw a swimming pool in the schoolyard nearby. "I'll go there," he said as he shook the flies off his back.

"Only a fool would choose the pool," said the others, traveling on.

The horse reached the pool. Just as he put one hoof in the smooth water, a man threw his boot. "Wait! Make room for me," cried the horse, zooming fast to catch up with his friends, "I have decided to come with you. That pool was full of tools and hoops."

My name is ______________________________.

Book

Moon

My name is ____________________________________.

Write **1** in the box if the name of the picture has a vowel sound as in **book**. Write **2** in the box if the name of the picture has a vowel sound as in **moon**.

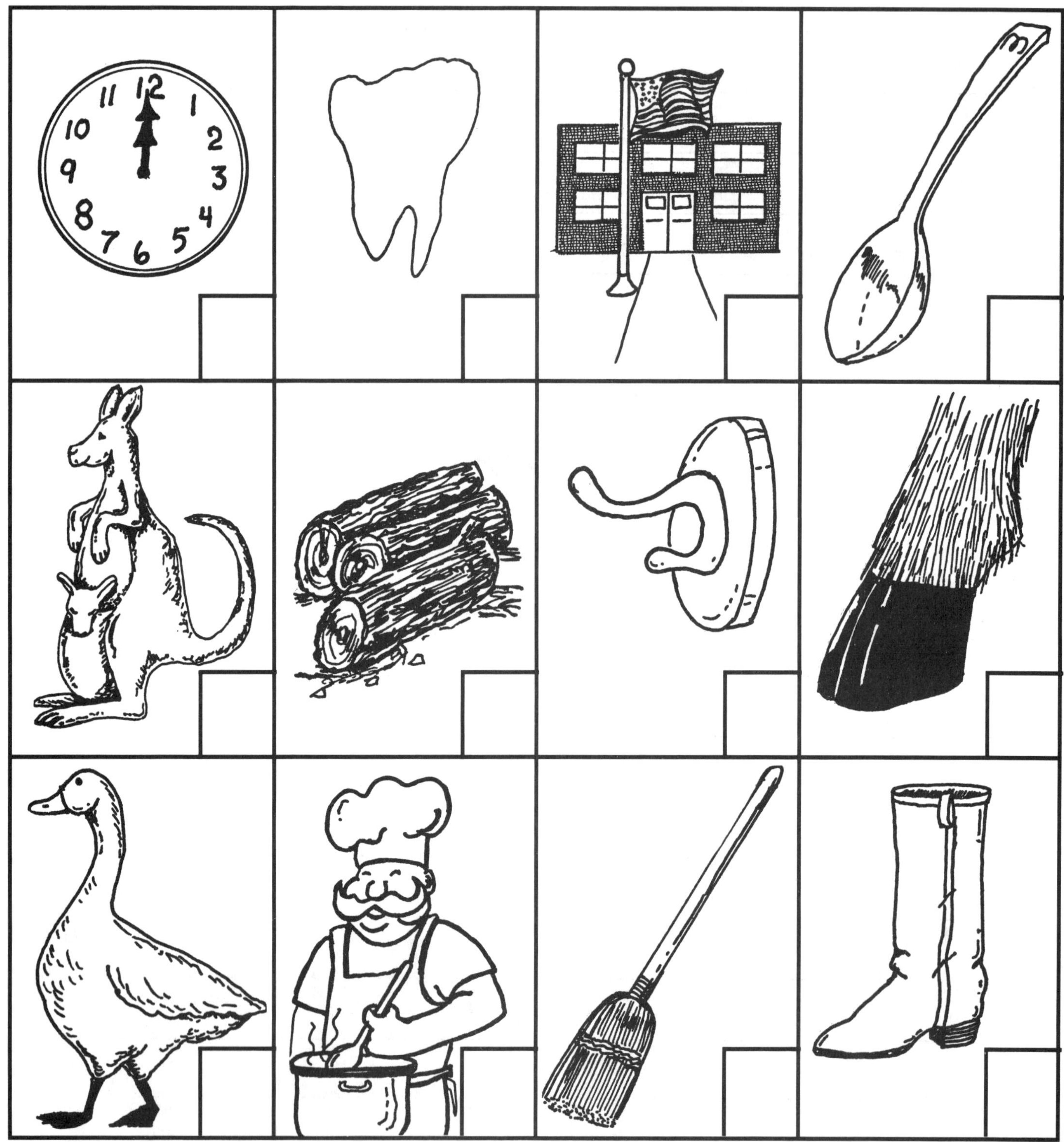

My name is ______________________.

Write the words from the list inside the key picture with the same special vowel sound.

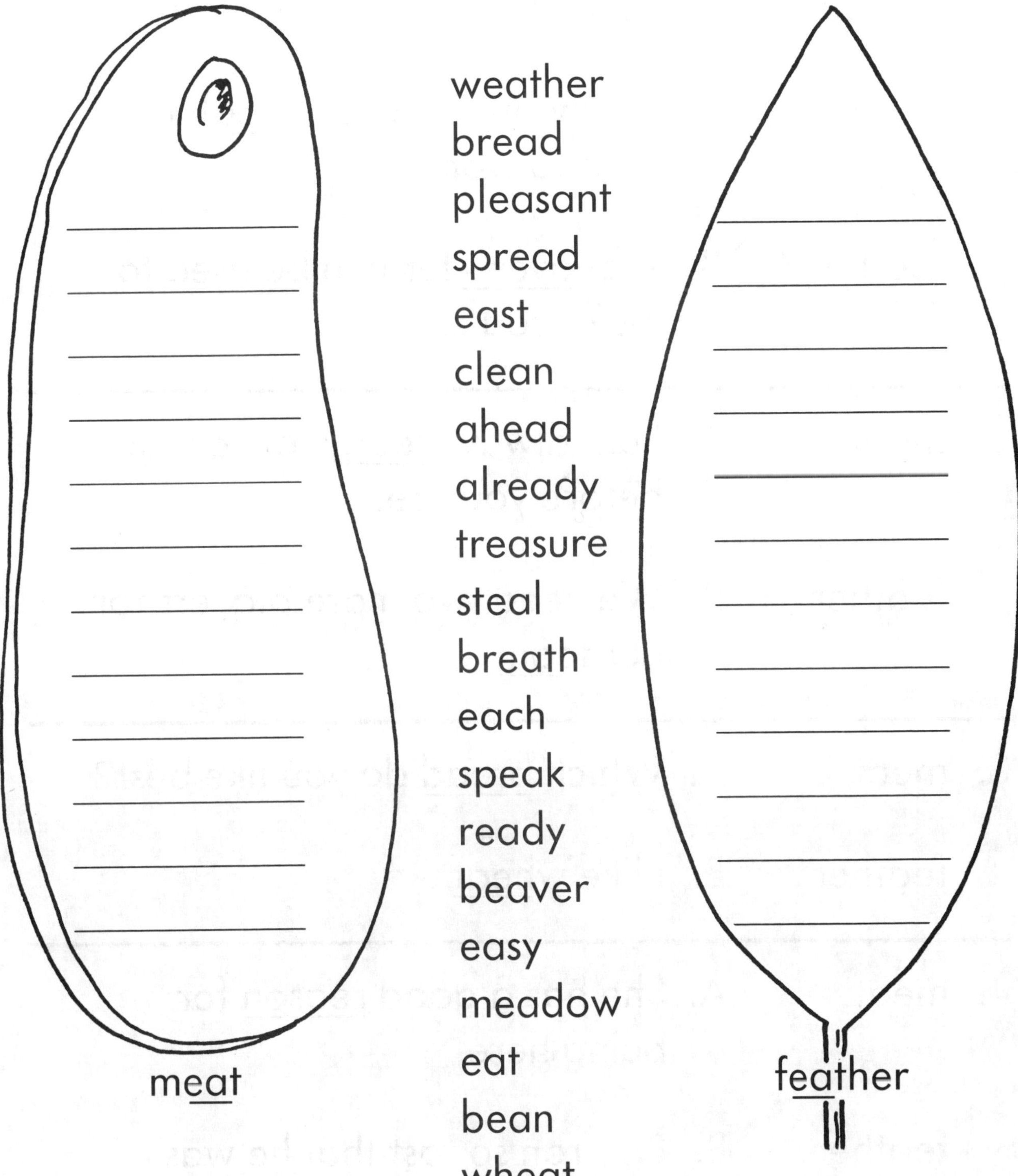

My name is ______________________________.

Draw a line from each key word to the sentence with an underlined word which has the same vowel sound.

1. meat — A. Dad wore his brown <u>leather</u> coat to work.

feather — B. A <u>beaver's</u> fur can be used to make coats.

---

2. meat — A. I am always <u>ready</u> for school before you are.

feather — B. We need two more players for our <u>team</u>.

---

3. meat — A. Which <u>bread</u> do you like best?

feather — B. I like <u>wheat</u>.

---

4. meat — A. She has a good <u>reason</u> for being here.

feather — B. Bob ran so fast that he was out of <u>breath</u>.

My name is ______________________________.

5. meat — A. Reach up high and get my green hat from the top shelf.

feather — B. Two of Pat's goldfish were dead.

---

6. meat — A. The divers found a treasure of gold.

feather — B. Leave us alone. We have to study for the test tomorrow.

---

7. meat — A. The soft radio music was pleasant to hear.

feather — B. The monkey's loud scream woke up every animal in the jungle.

---

8. meat — A. Breakfast, lunch, and dinner are meals.

feather — B. When you make your bed, put on your new spread.

My name is ________________________________.

9. meat — A. Joe was too <u>weak</u> to lift the huge boxes.

feather — B. Many black and white cows stood in the <u>meadow</u> eating grass.

---

10. meat — A. There is a piece of <u>thread</u> hanging from your coat.

feather — B. The sun rises in the <u>east</u> every morning.

---

11. meat — A. In some places the <u>weather</u> is always warm.

feather — B. "I will not <u>repeat</u> the question," said the announcer.

---

12. meat — A. The picture of an <u>eagle</u> is on a one dollar bill.

feather — B. <u>Already</u> you have written a three-page story!

My name is ____.

Write the letters on the lines to complete each sentence.

1. If you l_____n on the glass case, it might break. (au, ir, ea)

2. Smart people are often clev_____. (al, oo, er)

3. The squ_____rels built a large nest in the treetop. (ir, or, aw)

4. Put a knife, fork, and sp_____n at each person's place. (or, au, oo)

5. I need two balls of red y_____n to finish making my socks. (ur, ar, ea)

6. Cover your mouth when you y_____n. (aw, oo, ea)

My name is ______________________________.

7. "You may s______ve my dinner now," said the queen. (er, al, ar)

8. Carl h______t his leg when he tried to climb the high fence. (oo, au, ur)

9. The animals drank from the cool br______k. (or, ir, oo)

10. As we stood on the sh______e, several large ships passed by. (or, er, ea)

11. Aunt Ann t______ght me how to hammer a nail straight into the wood. (er, au, ea)

12. Sara held her h______d in her hands as she thought about the problem. (ir, al, ea)

My name is ____________________.

Circle the words in each row that have the same vowel sound as the first word.

1. third	gift	her	burn
2. look	good	tool	shook
3. eat	already	please	reach
4. horse	rooster	story	pony
5. hard	army	garden	star
6. talk	caught	crawl	take
7. dinner	over	fur	herd
8. room	spoon	wool	hook
9. head	weather	clean	ready
10. turn	dirty	barn	church

My name is ______________________________.

Circle the word that names the picture.

cloud
clown
clock

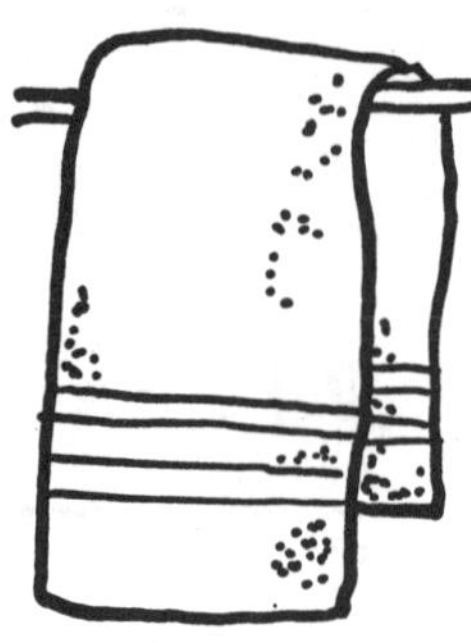

throw
towel
town

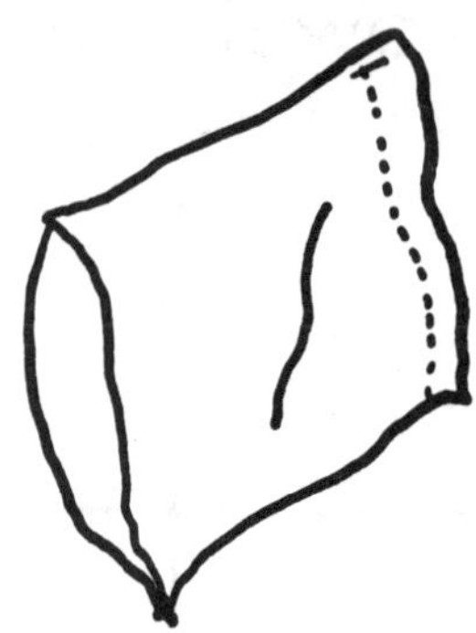

pillow
plow
poor

crow
crowd
crown

house
window
glass

own
owl
oil

bowl
bow
bow-wow

flow
floor
flower

arrow
airplane
apart

through
follow
throw

from
frown
form

shadow
show
tomorrow

My name is ______________________________.

Write the word on the line to answer each question.

low	allow	show
now	power	narrow
town	brown	shadow
plow	tower	swallow
crow	blows	tomorrow

1. Which word means to pass food from the mouth to the throat?

   ____

2. Which word names a bird not liked by farmers?

   ____

3. Which word means to let someone do something?

   ____

4. Which word names a high building?

   ____

My name is ________________________________.

5. Which word is the day after today?

____

6. Which word means not wide?

____

7. Which word means force or strength?

____

8. Which word means not high or tall?

____

9. Which word tells us what tractors can do to the ground? ______________________________

10. Which word tells us what the moving wind does?

____

My name is ______________________________.

Circle the word that has a vowel sound
like **cow** or **crow**.
Write yes on the line if the sentence is true.
Write no if it is not true.

1. Dogs and bears can growl. ________

2. A crowd is one person. ________

3. To borrow something means it is yours. ________

4. Babies are grown-up people. ________

5. Turtles and snails are slow. ________

6. May follows June. ________

7. Now means right away. ________

8. Snow feels hot and wet. ________

9. A clown is funny. ________

10. Something empty inside is hollow. ________

My name is ____.

Write the missing letters in the words below each picture. Find the words in the puzzle and circle them.

n____se

p____son

Word Hunt

cowb____

v	s	e	r	o	y	s	t	e	r
c	o	w	b	o	y	o	i	n	c
b	z	x	p	o	i	n	t	s	o
d	f	l	o	i	c	o	i	n	s
f	i	e	o	i	l	n	d	t	h
e	m	n	i	s	t	o	y	s	s
i	n	j	g	l	e	a	r	b	o
s	n	o	i	s	e	t	e	r	k
h	o	y	n	p	o	i	s	o	n
c	o	r	b	o	y	r	e	c	t
b	e	t	a	d	w	n	c	i	l

b____

____l

t____s

p____nt

c____ns

____ster

enj____

My name is ________________________________.

Write in the missing words.

oil	voice	join
boy	point	toys
joy	noise	coin
	cowboy	

1. I can be a penny or a dime. You take me when you go to the store. I am a ________________ .

2. I am on the end of a pencil. A pencil will not write without me. I am a ________________ .

3. I am happiness. I am fun. I am called ________________ .

4. I have a job. I spend most of my time outdoors. Sometimes I get very lonely. I am a ________________ .

5. Tops, dolls, trucks, trains, balls, jacks, marbles, and games. We are all ________________ .

6. You hear me when you speak and sing. I am your ________________ .

My name is ______________________________.

Special Vowel Sounds

shark  her  bird  fork

turtle  auto 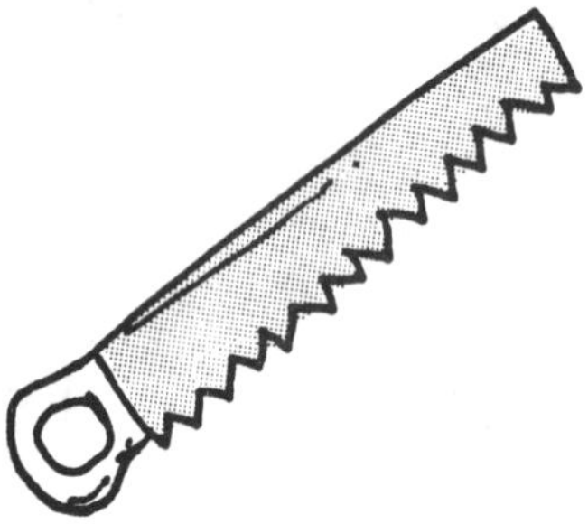 saw  ball

book 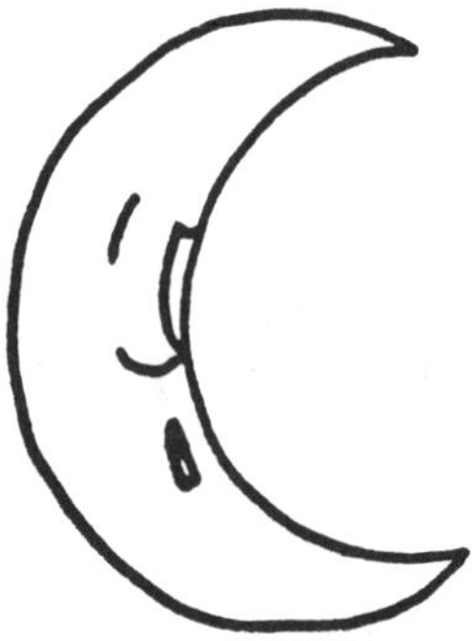 moon 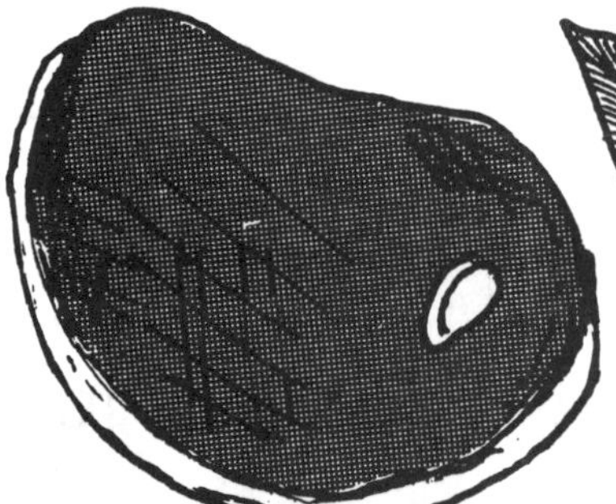 meat  feather

cow  crow  oil  boy

My name is ______________________________.

Label the pictures in each row.
Draw a large X on the picture that has the same vowel sound as the first word.

1. school

book
tools
home

_______________ _______________ _______________

2. feather

wreath
head
barn

_______________ _______________ _______________

3. over

numbers
balloons
scarf

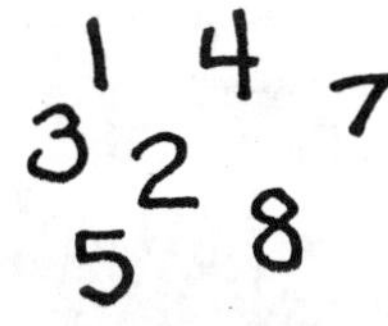

_______________ _______________ _______________

4. now

horn
tooth
down

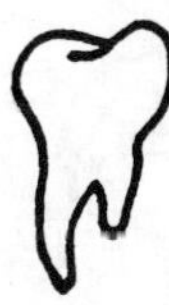

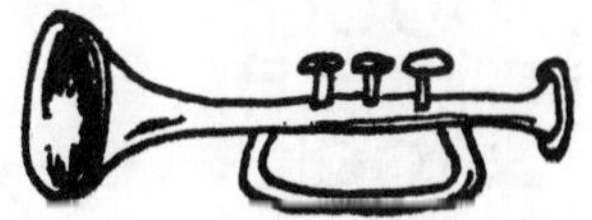

_______________ _______________ _______________

My name is ____.

5. horse

corn
claw
faucet

______________ ______________ ______________

6. ball

vowels
cards
talk

a e i o u

______________ ______________ ______________

7. third

candy
window
skirt

______________ ______________ ______________

8. bark

strawberry
arm
fire

______________ ______________ ______________

9. good

clock
bowl
cookies

______________ ______________ ______________

My name is ______________________________.

10. join

butterfly
cowboy
clown

_______ _______ _______

11. grow

snowman
owl
pot

_______ _______ _______

12. saw

crawl
ladder
star

_______ _______ _______

13. hurry

kangaroo
thermometer
paw

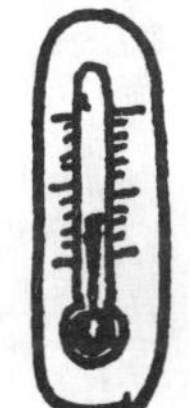

_______ _______ _______

14. eat

treasure
peas
forty

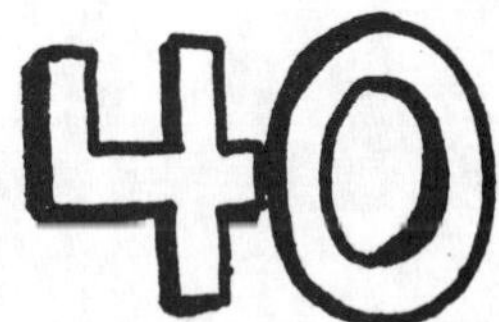

_______ _______ _______

My name is ______________________________.

Circle two words in each row that have the same vowel sound as the first word.

1. fall	caught	saw	floor
2. hard	farther	hurt	garden
3. blow	over	blue	own
4. shook	room	stood	hoof
5. head	mean	beg	ready
6. hurt	dirty	party	curb
7. for	fur	popcorn	store
8. toys	log	coins	boys
9. food	room	too	cook
10. first	fist	thirsty	teacher
11. how	town	flower	who
12. each	please	bread	easy

My name is ______________________________________.

Write these words under the key picture or pictures on the next page with the same special vowel sound.

whisper	tomorrow	purple
call	shadow	chart
large	enjoy	straw
more	spoon	stood
third	brown	steal
pool	point	sister
crowd	bread	thread
ready	boot	salt
good	east	morning
	caught	

My name is ______________________________.

My name is ______________________________________.

Vowel Sound Tic-Tac-Toe

A.

B.

C.

D.

E.

F.

Dear Parent or Guardian:

We have just completed the final unit of *Phonics in Context* in the program *INSIGHTS: Reading as Thinking*. This unit reviews the fourteen special vowel sounds we focused on this year.

Your child might enjoy starting a diary or daily record of events or perhaps just a list of books that the two of you have read. New books might be compared and contrasted with the books on the list. Diary entries can be great fun to read over even a month after they were written.

Now that the school year is ending, I hope that you can see the difference that *INSIGHTS* has made in your child's progress toward becoming a successful and enthusiastic reader.

Sincerely,

Your Child's Teacher

Literature List

Dragonwagon, Crescent. *The Itch Book.* Macmillan, 1990. Find out what happens on a hot day in the Ozarks when the heat makes everyone itch.

Freeman, Don. *Norman the Doorman.* Viking, 1959. An art museum mouse creates his masterpiece and enters it anonymously in a sculpture contest.

Gramatky, Hardie. *Little Toot.* Putnam, 1939. The classic story of a young tug who saves the day.

Kellogg, Steven. *Chicken Little.* Morrow, 1985. Foxy Loxy impersonates a police officer and, thanks to Sergeant Hippo Hefty, justice finally prevails.

Ness, Evaline. *Sam, Bangs, and Moonshine.* Holt, 1966. When Samantha tells Thomas a lie that endangers his life, she finally learns the hard way the difference between real and moonshine.

Walsh, Ellen Stoll. *Mouse Count.* Harcourt, 1991. A hungry snake and ten clever mice make an exciting counting adventure.

Yashima, Taro. *Crow Boy.* Viking, 1955. Caldecott Award Honor Book. Chibi, an outcast boy in his Japanese village school, proves his value to his unkind classmates.